Hesburgh of Notre Dame
Priest, Educator, Public Servant

Hesburgh of Notre Dame
Priest, Educator, Public Servant

John C. Lungren, Jr.

Sheed & Ward

Sheed & Ward™ is a service of National Catholic Reporter Publishing, Inc.

Library of Congress Catalog Card Number: 86-64003

ISBN: 1-55612-102-4

Published by: Sheed & Ward
               115 E. Armour Blvd. P.O. Box 414292
               Kansas City, MO 64141-0281

To order, call: (800) 821-7926

Contents

Dedication

For my father, John Charles Lungren, M.D., truly a priest as both father and physician.

For my Mother, Lorain Kathleen Lungren, whose soul magnifies the Lord.

ACKNOWLEDGEMENTS

Shakespeare writes " Blessed are you whose worthiness gives scope . . ." Such lives compel attention and give great pleasure to observe. This has been my experience in writing about Theodore Hesburgh's life and career.

His life and career include priest, university president, educator, chairman of congressional commissions and private foundations, Vatican envoy to an international agency, member of the National Science Board and President Ford's Clemency Board, and patron of a great artist's sculpture. These provide but a brief index to the range and breadth of his contributions to Notre Dame, the Church, and civil government.

In order to encompass the full scope of Father Hesburgh's career and interests, I interviewed a number of individuals—his brother, colleagues, friends and independent observers who gave special insights into his life and character. Moreover, I was able to interview Hesburgh himself at length at the home of his brother in Pacific Palisades, California.

Among the independent observers were members and staff of the U.S. Commission on Civil Rights and President Ford's Clemency Board, the executive director of the Select Commission on Immigration, two reporters from *The New York Times*, two former university presidents, a former chief executive officer of a major U.S. corporation, the former President of Venezuela and the Vatican's former Apostolic Delegate to the United States.

Finally, this book would never have been written and published were it not for the loving inspiration and dedication of my wife, Nancy. She tenaciously encouraged me, transcribed the interview tapes, and provided an editor's necessary discipline and insight. I am deeply grateful to her.

John C. Lungren, Jr.

For men become myths, not by what they
know, nor even by what they achieve,
but by the tasks they set for themselves.

—Henry Kissinger
A World Restored

We do not display greatness by going to
one extreme, but in touching both at once,
and filling all the intervening space.

—Pascal
Pensées

You are a priest forever according to
the order of Melchizedek.

—Old Testament Psalmist
Psalm 110

FOREWORD

"Entrust your works to the Lord, and your plans will succeed." This verse from the Book of Proverbs (16:3) provides a window on the world of Theodore M. Hesburgh, C.S.C. The most successful university president in the history of 20th century American higher education is a man of deep religious faith. He entrusted both himself and his works to the Lord; the Lord did not disappoint him.

As a member of the Congregation of Holy Cross, Father Hesburgh's spirituality reflects the values and the cross of Christ. People who look at the world from a different perspective, and who also know Father Hesburgh, cannot fully understand his style, candor, availability, and commitment to the promotion of just relationships in the world community. He is, after all, the chief executive officer of a complex institution. His influence is felt in the power centers around the world. He could, some say, have been a great success in business or government. Or, as the same point is made by others in the form of a secular lament, what a misuse of manpower on the part of a church which lacked the vision to make him a bishop!

Some actually urged him to run for the U.S. Senate from his native state of New York after Robert Kennedy's assassination. Many admire the ease with which he moves in the circles of the wealthy and powerful, but remain puzzled by his apparent decision to remove himself from the personal appropriation of wealth or power.

In the ready but complicated world of mid-century America, Theodore Hesburgh emerged as an uncomplicated and uncompromising man who converted the presidency of the University of Notre Dame into a "bully pulpit" and, in the process, moved his university into the front ranks of American higher education. None of this for personal gain; all of it for love of the Catholic church and his religious community within which he answered a call to priesthood, the central focus of his life.

In connection with a story timed to coincide with the announcement of the selection of Father Hesburgh's successor to the Notre Dame presidency, I received a telephone call from the *Boston Globe*. The reporter asked for my estimate of the Hesburgh contribution to American and Catholic higher education. I suggested that Father Hesburgh was the top leader in higher education and had, during his 35-year tenure as Notre Dame's chief executive officer, shown admirable staying power. He demonstrated, I said, that one can manage a simultaneous commitment to persons and to institutions. I thought the point worth making in an age of skepticism about the value of institutional commitments. In any case, the interviewer either misheard or miswrote and quoted me in print as saying that the subject of his story was a man committed to both "passions and institutions." Not too wide of the mark, actually. He is a man with passions for excellence, for peace and justice, and, most of all, for priesthood. His place in the history of the church in America and in its apostolate of education is assured. His ability to stand out in an age of secularization as a citizen-priest reflecting credit on both sides of that hyphen may prove to be his most significant achievement.

The Hesburgh intelligence, energy level, capacity for work and interest in issues that shape the lives of people remain awesome after seven decades of his own membership in the human community. Life has afforded him the opportunity to stretch his talents fully. He was obviously overextended at times, but never unable to manage his responsibilities. An anecdote will illustrate that point.

I remember receiving a frantic phone call from one of Father Hesburgh's close assistants a month or two before the scheduled opening of the National Congress on Church-Related Colleges and Universities in 1978. Notre Dame was the site; Father Hesburgh was the announced keynoter along with Duke University President Terry Sanford. Organizer and prime mover of the event was John D. Moseley, former president of Austin College in Sherman, Texas, who had enlisted me to help with the planning. The Notre Dame President was overseas on an ambassadorial assignment relating to an international conference on science and technology. His staff was nervous because there was no evidence that a speech was ready; indeed there was some doubt as to whether the speaker had a clear idea of what he was expected to say. Could I help? I drafted a short speech and sent it out to South Bend with a note indicating that it would be enough to "get him down the runway and into the air," he could adjust the controls after takeoff.

When we had dinner together on campus just before the opening session of the National Congress, Father Hesburgh thanked me for the text, said he had read it several times but was not going to use it. It helped him focus his own thoughts and write his own speech two days before. He then went on to explain that with the single exception of a St. Patrick's Day talk, drafted by one of his conferees ("I'm sure my Irish mother will forgive me for that!"), the busy president of Notre Dame had never delivered a speech which he had not written.

It is quite unlikely that he will ever write an autobiography. Hence the value of a biography like this one which helps to document the record of a truly remarkable career.

William J. Byron, S.J.
President
Catholic University of America

PREFACE

No biography of Ted Hesburgh can be "definitive" at least while he is alive and in orbit. Now that the time has come for him to pass the baton to a successor at Notre Dame it might seem appropriate to take an accounting. But that leaves unguessed and unspoken what he is going to be "when he grows up." In no way is it imaginable that he will retire to a secluded, monastic life. It was once said of the great civil libertarian, Roger Baldwin, that if ever his goals were achieved, you would see a sign outside his office saying "martyr for hire." So too with Ted Hesburgh—as long as there is any indecency, oppression, poverty, or inequity in the world, he will be suited up and ready to take it on. His jutting jaw and unblinking eyes will let you know that eagerness is matched by toughness and determination. "Scrappy," in a slightly Cagneyesque way, is part of his style; tenacious and bold, although free of braggadocio. President Nixon found this out when Father Hesburgh was on the Civil Rights Commission. General Walt was to learn what a tough adversary he was on the post-Vietnam clemency panel.

Unlike many crusaders for their causes, however, Ted Hesburgh knows the world progresses by consensus only. He masters the art of forging agreement among those who are prone to disagree. Representing the Vatican on atomic energy and weapons in the first conclave of East and West nations, he was made more credible as a broker because his "nation" had no atomic bombs. His effort to create a joint centre in Jerusalem for all Eastern and Western religions is the one bright spot in a city where all religious inheritance is betrayed by violence and hatred. His belief in amnesty, tempered by realism and the need for consensus, brought President Ford's clemency board through a bitter dispute to a humane conclusion that served both the anguished individuals and the wounded nation well.

When the Rockefeller Foundation had to find a new president to succeed John Knowles, there were so many headstrong factions that only Ted Hesburgh could be entrusted to lead the search. His strength is not neutrality or the art of compromise; it lies, rather, in the trust of those affected. Part of this trust is due to respect for his idealism. A larger part, I think, is because he does not let his own ego get between the problem and its solution.

The crisis, politely called "student unrest," in the late sixties showed both Ted Hesburgh's national "clout" and his astute ingenuity. He saved the campuses, (as well as President Nixon) from the disastrous suggestion that the student problem be handled by bringing the FBI onto the campus in the name of law and order. Hesburgh's message to Governor Rockefeller at the Governors' Conference was the finger in the dyke that prevented this breakdown of all constitutional restraint. Given the student mood of the time, such folly could have meant civil strife. Also, the famous Hesburgh early warning ultimatum to students who persisted in violence or disruption, was an amalgam of fairness and firmness, typical of his educational leadership.

Such instances of national leadership were dramatic and visible to those who cared about their own students or their own institution. But the heart of Father Hesburgh's educational aspiration and achievement is found at home in South Bend. A tour of the campus with the President as your guide is a revelation of the accomplishment and of the man and his deep commitment to Notre Dame. The bricks and mortar are impressive. But the spirit of the place is evidenced in all its corners, buildings and plazas, its faculty and especially its students. There is no public sullenness.

It is easy to say Father Ted holds Notre Dame together in high spirit and high spirituality—easy because it is in large part true. I would call it "purposeful optimism." It is not the "great glad boy" optimism; rather it sees that with a sense of purpose, problems can be overcome. It is not purposeful in the sense of grim determination. Rather it is a purpose gathered from without, from a sense of enjoyment of accomplishment in the world around you, making it in some small way better.

The spirit of purposeful optimism infuses all that Ted Hesburgh has done.

Kingman Brewster
Master
Oxford University

CHAPTER 1
SERVING IN THE OIKOUMENÉ

In northern Indiana where the fierce winters have hardened generations of European immigrants, lies a university founded by a French priest. Today it exits as an aspired fruition of an immigrant Church and as an intellectual pilgrimage that transcended its own parochial beginnings.

The University of Notre Dame emerged out of the intellectual wilderness of an immigrant American Catholicism and into the tradition of those great universities of the Middle Ages—Paris, Oxford, Cambridge, Bologna, Salamanca, and Louvain. There, philosophy and theology confronted contemporary thought and the cardinal characteristic of the great medieval universities was a quest for knowledge as an integral whole. It was not an etymological coincidence for the medieval Christian mind that "whole" and "holy" came from the same Old English root, *hál,* meaning "sound," "uninjured," or "healthy."

St. Thomas Aquinas offered a magisterial expression of the organic nature of knowledge in his Summa Theologica. "For all things that exist," he wrote, "are seen to be ordered to each other

1

since some serve others.'' In his synthesis of Greek philosophy Aquinas mediated the philosophy of Aristotle, creating a Christian philosophy which could reconcile ancient wisdom and modern modalities.

Since the Middle Ages, this intellectual tradition has weakened. Some observers such as George Bernard Shaw have even said that ''a Catholic university is a contradiction in terms.'' However, Notre Dame has belied such false assumptions and has witnessed the appearance of a truly renaissance figure in the person of its retiring president, Theodore Martin Hesburgh. Theodore Hesburgh was president of the University of Notre Dame for thirty-five years— he became the university's 16th president in 1952 at the age of 35—a generation in which he led the school not only to its pre-eminent position among Catholic universities, but also into the very front ranks of the great American universities. (In fact, in October 1986, Hesburgh was named the nation's most effective college president in a survey of 485 academics.) Yet these achievements—however extraordinary in themselves — do not fully encompass the varied dimensions of this singular and perceptive priest's career.

As Chairman of the United States Commission on Civil Rights he exercised the moral leadership that guided the commission and the nation for 14 years until he was dismissed by President Nixon in 1972 for being too forceful and unyielding in the pursuit of equal rights for the oppressed minorities in the nation.

Appointed by President Ford to the Clemency Board, he argued for a compassionate and just approach in granting clemency to Vietnam draft evaders and deserters with such an eloquent and commanding presence that he became the board's conscience, and it was he whom the other board members would turn to when they were undecided.

His famous 15-minute ''cease and desist'' order during the campus rebellions of 1969 led the way for other university presidents in handling campus disorders. Less well known is his cable to Governor Rockefeller at the Governor's Conference of 1969 opposing federal legislation to regulate student behavior. As a result, President Nixon was dissuaded from extending federal police power to the nation's campuses.

In 1974 Hesburgh delivered the prestigious Terry Lectures at Yale, the first Catholic university president so honored, succeeding in the lecture chair such distinguished scientists, philosophers, and theologians as Carl Jung, John Dewey, George Gaylord Simpson, Robert Millikan, Reinhold Niebuhr, Paul Tillich, and Jacques Maritain. Hesburgh's lectures, published as *The Humane Imperative: A Challenge for the Year 2000,* are the Christian humanist's visionary reflections ranging from the hermeneutics of the Kingdom of God to the Green Revolution.

As Chairman of the Overseas Development Council he helped influence U.S. policy—official and unofficial—in resolving the world food shortage and formulating measures to achieve economic and social justice in the Third and Fourth World countries. In fact Secretary of State Cyrus Vance, aware that Hesburgh's international expertise and prestige would be an invaluable asset for American diplomacy, offered him two positions during the Carter Administration. The diplomatic posts—which Hesburgh declined with regret—were Undersecretary of State for Latin American Affairs and at-large ambassador to the Third and Fourth World nations (this latter appointment would have been a new position in the State Department).

Hesburgh did accept a diplomatic post in November 1977, when he became U.S. Ambassador and Chairman of the U.S. Delegation to the United Nations Conference on Science and Technology for Development.

Among the myriad awards and honorary degrees are three of the highest citations which can be conferred upon a citizen, educator, and religious leader: President Johnson awarded him the U.S. Medal of Freedom in 1964 for "his wisdom in the struggle of the rights of man," the American Association of University Professors gave him the Meiklejohn Award in 1970 for his contributions to academic freedom, and in 1972 he received the Reinhold Niebuhr Award for his contributions to religious freedom.

On May 22, 1977, President Carter delivered a major foreign policy address at Notre Dame, opening the speech in praise of Hesburgh's eloquent advocacy of human rights. "In his 25 years as president of Notre Dame," the President began, "Father Hesburgh has spoken more consistently and effectively in support of the rights of human beings than any American I know."

The accuracy of the President's statement was amply affirmed a week later by *The New York Times*, which covered an NBC News special debate between three Americans and three English-speaking Russians on the subject of human rights held at Georgetown University. The three Americans were Alan Dershowitz, a Harvard Law School professor, Robert G. Kaiser, former Moscow Bureau Chief for *The Washington Post*, and Hesburgh. The *Times* noted in its review of the 90-minute debate that "the Russians did not fare well against Father Hesburgh's projection of basic human decency . . ."

Hesburgh was permanent Vatican City representative to the International Atomic Energy Agency from 1957 to 1970 and a member of the National Science Board from 1954 to 1966. He has been chairman of the Rockefeller Foundation, a director of the Chase Manhattan Bank and a member of the Carnegie Commission on the Future of Higher Education. He has been president of both the Association of American Colleges and the International Federation of Catholic Universities, a trustee of the United Negro College Fund, and chairman of the Business-Higher Education Forum.

Dr. Franklin Murphy has known Hesburgh for over 30 years dating back to when Murphy was chancellor at the University of Kansas. A medical doctor (he was dean of the medical school at Kansas), Murphy is cast in the same mold as Hesburgh—a man of wide-ranging intellectual interests who is an efficient and effective administrator. Appointed chancellor of the University of California at Los Angeles in 1960, Murphy guided the school through the turbulent 60's. Murphy is a retired chairman of the board of Times-Mirror Company, one of the largest corporate publishing enterprises in the nation. In describing Hesburgh, Murphy says, "Ted is a handsome, vigorous, energetic human being who exudes physical vitality and energy. But when you cut through the surface—get down to the man himself—you find a person of unlimited integrity, a remarkable amount of objectivity, an extremely intelligent and enormously sensitive person who is more concerned about the rest of the world than he is about himself."

Unlike many influential leaders whose extraordinary gifts usually struggle with the ego's desire for recognition, Hesburgh has, according to Murphy, sublimated and directed his ego beyond himself. "I think there is little or no ego in Ted. Let's be realistic—no matter whether a person is a priest or a prince there is some ego. But in Ted's case there's not the kind of ego that says I want to be the most visible or the most important," he explains.

Murphy believes Hesburgh is truly driven by the Christian summons to serve others in the *oikoumené*—that is serving the inhabited world with an unreserved commitment. "You know it sounds kind of fancy and romantic but with Ted it's really true. The interesting thing is that it is combined in Ted—this desire to make the world a better place and to make people better people—this philosophical notion is combined with a sense of pragmatism that is concerned not just with the goal but with the ability and knowledge to actually accomplish it."

Hesburgh's concern for others can be seen, according to Murphy, in the way he spends his free time. "I've been to many conferences with Ted overseas and he would go into a country—Chile, Peru, Brazil, or whatever—and attend all the meetings and even do the social things. But it was obvious that he was up much earlier than the rest of us and he went to bed much later because he was always visiting people outside of the conference. His whole theory is 'How can you talk about a country if you don't know its people?' "

C.R. Smith, former chairman of the board and president of American Airlines, has spent almost every Christmas with Hesburgh for

over the past 20 years. During the Christmas of 1976 they traveled
to Africa and, before the death of Richfield Oil President Charles
Jones, stayed with Jones and his family at his home in Baja, California. Smith first met Hesburgh as a member of the business advisory
council of Notre Dame's Business School, having been invited to
become a member by a former Notre Dame student. Arriving at the
university for his first council meeting, Smith met Hesburgh and was
immediately impressed by the "unusual, sparkling personality and
friendly attitude of the good Father."

"Your first impression is that he is interested in *you*, which of
course, compels attention," Smith says. "Second, he is willing to discuss nearly any subject you may choose and you are likely to find
him better informed than you are. He possesses a burning sense of
curiosity—he never finds a subject in which he is not interested.
He is something of a perfectionist. Whatever he does he insists on
doing well. People who meet the good Father do not forget him.
And, for long-term friendships, he lives up to expectations."

Two of Hesburgh's colleagues on the Civil Rights Commission witnessed the catholic nature of his interests. "His appetite for reading knows no bounds. He is the most interesting person I've ever
met," says Civil Rights Commission Vice-Chairman Dr. Stephen
Horn. Former Commission Staff Director Howard Glickstein recalls
an incident in Mexico City which reveals Hesburgh's renaissance
personality. "I once happened to be in Mexico City at the same time
he was," Glickstein remembers. "One evening he was addressing
the Notre Dame Club of Mexico City and he invited me to come
along. He spoke about what the world was going to be like in the
year 2000 covering every conceivable field of knowledge—
philosophy, theology, physics. He had a little index card in front of
him and discoursed for an hour. It was one of the most comprehensive talks I've ever heard ranging over the entire spectrum of human
knowledge."

G.K. Chesterton once wrote that "the world is too serious to be
taken seriously." Hesburgh possesses the kind of well-developed and

ironic sense of humor needed in such an unduly solemn milieu. In a letter written to Vice President Agnew in 1969 concerning the campus revolts, Hesburgh took note of the mournful political mien of the day and commented, ''. . . a measure of humor would help from time to time to break up the deathly seriousness of the present scene.'' Horn has seen Hesburgh in deadly serious circumstances such as his confrontations with the Nixon Administration over civil rights and was impressed with the sense of perspective Hesburgh always kept about himself and the situation at hand. ''I think one of the most impressive things about him,'' Horn says, ''is his sense of humor.''

CBS television reporter Dan Rather caught the satiric edge of Hesburgh's wit in an interview he conducted with Hesburgh for a profile on CBS's *Who's Who?* The profile began with Hesburgh and Rather arriving on a plane at the South Bend airport where they were met by the university's limousine. Inside the car Rather asked Hesburgh a few questions as they were being driven to the campus. Reaching into his investigative repertory, Rather attempted to hurl one of his reputed ''zingers'' at Hesburgh by asking, ''Do you always ride around in such style?'' Hesburgh looked at the well-known reporter with quizzical amusement for a moment and then replied: ''No, only when I greet such distinguished visitors as President Carter or Dan Rather.'' Rather grinned sheepishly and said nothing.

Later, in Hesburgh's office, Rather again attempted to catch Hesburgh off-guard with another question designed to embarrass. ''Before you became a priest,'' Rather asked, ''did you ever raise hell . . . I mean did you ever chase the girls or drink too much on occasion?'' Hesburgh looked at Rather directly with his dark brown eyes, a slight smile of amusement again flickering over his face, and said: ''Well, we all chased the girls when we were young . . . but I think we did it in a more modest way than is done now.''

Smith remembers when a group of students came to Hesburgh demanding that the annual selection of homecoming queen be abolished because they believed the event had become a sexist symbol perpetuating the oppression of women. ''The good Father said that he found it difficult to select a young woman without some attention to sex," Smith recalls, "but he added that he might work out some arrangement by which Notre Dame could go along. Noting that the campus was flooded with *Playboy,* a magazine which, he said, was certainly not without some sex symbols, Hesburgh suggested that perhaps the students would like to first remove the girlie magazines from campus dormitories and thereafter he would be prepared to discuss abolishing the homecoming queen."

The late Charles Jones used to tell friends that Hesburgh's presence at his Baja home during Christmas in no way inhibited his robust propensity for punctuated language or an occasional drink. "During my long friendship with C.R. Smith, I had seen little evidence of strong religious devotion and I was very much surprised when I heard from Smith that a Catholic priest had been invited to share Christmas with us," Jones said. "I readily saw an end of our out-of-door conversational language and believed his presence might interfere with our habit of having a drink from time to time. However, it turned out that Smith did my family and me an unusual favor, introducing us to one of the finest men I have ever met."

CHAPTER 2
FAMILY AND EARLY LIFE:
REMARKABLE
SELF-POSSESSION

The future priest and university president was born on May 25, 1917 in Syracuse, New York. He was the second of five children in a middle-class Catholic family that descended from the great influx of mid-19th century German, French, and Irish immigrants. His father, Theodore B. V., was the son of third-generation French and German immigrants. His mother, Anne Marie, was of Irish descent (Murphy) and was educated in New York private schools by German nuns. She was a bright, vivacious woman who made her home and family the focal point of her life.

The roots of great achievement are often found in the antecedent influence of parents and grandparents. Hesburgh's career is no exception. His ability to educate and to write and speak with considerable eloquence can perhaps be traced to his paternal grandfather, Theodore Bernard Hesburgh.

A school teacher by vocation, his grandfather later became an editorial columnist for the *New York World* under the pen name "Knickerbocker." (Today, several generations later, his grandson contributes occasional essays on civil rights, education, politics and foreign policy to the editorial pages of the *New York Times*. The wide-ranging essays written by his grandfather for the *World* from 1885 to 1906 were reflected later in Hesburgh's intellectual interests and social concerns. The subjects "Knickerbocker" explored, and on which he expatiated, included politics, religion, economics, education, medicine, marriage, and the theater. He wrote columns concerning such men as Henry George, Samuel Tilden, Grover Cleveland, Theodore Roosevelt, William Jennings Bryan, and John D. Rockefeller. A profound sympathy for the impoverished and oppressed pervaded the essays which discussed such social and moral issues as child labor, French anti-Semitism, the plight of Pennsylvania coal miners, the massacre of Jews in Russia, and the destruction of cotton crops to prevent price declines.

In 1886 (a little over two decades before Hesburgh's birth in 1917), his grandfather wrote a column in the *World* which was a remarkable prediction of his future grandson's career.

George's reformist economic theories had provoked considerable controversy in the 1880's, especially his "single-tax" proposal which would have eliminated all taxes except one to be levied on property owners. The disparity between the rich and the poor would be effaced, according to George, by returning the money earned by landowners to those whose labor had increased the land's value. The Catholic Church, a large landowner, looked upon George and his proposal with trepidation. In fact, New York Archbishop Michael Corrigan excommunicated Father McGlynn for his active support of George. (Cardinal James Gibbons of Baltimore later intervened with the Vatican and in 1892 the ecclesiastical ban was lifted.)

In his column, "Knickerbocker" censured Archbishop Corrigan for suspending McGlynn and allowing him to be summoned "to Rome to appear before the Propaganda." Also, he noted that the chancellor of the New York Archdiocese had sent a letter denouncing McGlynn to a Tammany Hall official. In concluding the essay, "Knickerbocker" spoke of the urgent need for an informative moral vision in politics, a vision which could best be supplied by "priestly savants." Then in a passage which actually prefigures the life of his grandson, the grandfather wrote:

> Cardinal Richelieu, the wily but illustrious minister of France, the shrewdest statesman of his time, was only a Carmelite priest. Archbishop Hughes (John Hughes, Archbishop of New York in the middle of the 19th century) was often consulted upon affairs of State by President Lincoln, during the trying times of his administration, and was rated a sagacious counsellor. Would not the great political and social problems of the age receive a clearer solution if some of the gigantic minds enclosed within the sacred precincts of the monastery were permitted to give free utterance to their vast accumulation of statesmanship?
>
> Surely the present corrupt and destructive political methods of government would in time be swept into oblivion were clergymen of decided honorable intentions to assume a strong and wholesome activity in the conduct of public affairs.

The upbringing of Hesburgh's father is a reflection of inherited tenacity which enabled his son to remain the head of a great American university during radical social, political, and economic transformations,—a time when most of Hesburgh's peers have been forced out of office or have resigned due to sheer enervation and frustration. (In the inside pocket of his suit coat Hesburgh keeps a list of 90 university presidents who have been driven from office since the 1960's. He has been known to take the list out and read it before a startled listener like a litany of early Church martyrs in the acute awareness that he is one of the last survivors.)

When Theodore B. V. Hesburgh was four years old, he lost his mother, brother and sister in the New York City flu epidemic of 1891. This nearly shattered his father, who decided to send his son to live with a large family of distant relatives on a farm in Iowa. There young Theodore learned to fend for himself and become independent very early in life. He used to say of this experience: "You can imagine what came to me at the dinner table being the eleventh and youngest child and the most distant relative."

At age six, an aunt from Staten Island brought him back to New York where, still having to fight his own battles, he worked for a bowling alley after school setting pins. He bought all of his own clothes at the age of 10. Although he went to high school, he virtually educated himself. Anticipating graduation and unable to afford college, he enrolled in an evening business school and, after six weeks when the teacher became ill, he was selected to teach the very class he was taking. Upon graduation from high school he went to work for the Pittsburgh Plate Glass Company in New York City as an office clerk and then became a salesman in upstate New York. He was eventually sent to Syracuse where he covered the whole state selling paint and glass. Having an instinctive business acumen, he recommended that the company set up a warehouse facility in central New York. When Pittsburgh Plate Glass approved, he selected the property and built the warehouse in Syracuse, where he managed it for 25 years.

Hesburgh's passion for his work, which is manifested by 20-hour days beginning at 7 a.m. and ending at 3 a.m., was perhaps also inherited from his father. His younger brother Jim, 52, recalls their father: "His main interest was in his work—I remember even to the point where every Sunday morning as a child I would go to the Post Office with him and pick up the mail. We would then go into the office and Dad would stay there for two hours after Mass and open the mail and check over the warehouse."

The elder Hesburgh passed on to his children a deep religious faith. Jim Hesburgh remembers that their father was a very conscientious and moral individual whose religion was very important to him. He believes that a lot of what his older brother is today has its roots in their father because "he was a great man to admire. He was very honest. He led a very full life. He was very proud, but at the same time very humble."

Hesburgh's boyhood possessed the kind of values and achievements expected by third-generation descendents of German and Irish immigrants. When he attended parochial schools he served as an altar boy, built model airplanes, hunted, fished, became a Life Scout, and once played Christ in a school passion play. By age 12 he had developed a remarkable self-possession. According to a 1960 *Time* magazine cover story on Hesburgh's life, young Hesburgh was asked by a priest what he wanted to be when he grew up. Hesburgh quickly dismissed the priest's proffered suggestions—fireman, policeman, explorer—and replied with absolute conviction, "I'm going to be a priest, Father. Like you." The priest, Father Thomas Duffy, a member of the Holy Cross order, was so impressed by the young boy's vocational certitude that he wrote his name down on a piece of paper, noting "fine boy, bright," and started encouraging him to attend Notre Dame.

Graduating third in his high school class, Hesburgh entered Notre Dame in 1934 and after a year on campus went to the Holy Cross novitiate at Rolling Prairie, Indiana. For 12 austere months, he arose every morning at 5 a.m., prayed and studied in Latin, cut down trees, built a silo, and maintained the rule of silence for 22 hours a day. It was certainly not the normal sojourn for a college sophomore and Hesburgh concedes that the novitiate was not unlike a military boot camp. The year was not easy for the gregarious Hesburgh ("I liked dancing. I liked everything," he told *Time*), but he endured it with his singular tenacity to be a priest. As he explained to the *Time* magazine correspondent, "I thought there was something more to life. By really belonging to nobody except God, you belong to everybody."

In his junior year Hesburgh was sent to the Gregorian University in Rome where he studied theology for three years. The brightest priests and seminarians in the Catholic Church throughout the world are sent to the Gregorian to study. In the cosmopolitan atmosphere where disparate cultures meshed with each other, Hesburgh began to learn many languages, assimilating French in the dormitory and absorbing Italian in street conversations. (He is also fluent in Spanish, German, and of course, Latin, and has a working knowledge of Russian, Portuguese, Greek, Hebrew, and Japanese.) Hesburgh was supposed to study in Rome for eight years in order to get a doctorate in philosophy and theology. However, when the war broke out during his first year of theology he returned to Washington, D.C., where he studied at Holy Cross College at Catholic University. After being ordained at Notre Dame in 1943, Hesburgh went on to receive his doctorate in theology at Washington.

Returning to Notre Dame in 1945 to teach theology, Hesburgh also took on extra duties such as becoming chaplain to the married veterans inundating the campus. As chaplain of ''Vetville,'' Hesburgh baptized babies, persuaded obstetricians to deliver at reduced rates, and babysat at his own discount fee of a sandwich and a cold glass of beer.

In 1948 he became head of the theology department and the next year he was named executive vice president at age 32. Hesburgh recounted what happened next with the self-effacing modesty that is one of his salient traits, ''In 1952 I became president of Notre Dame and I've been stuck with that ever since. That's the whole story of my life.''

CHAPTER 3
HESBURGH AND NOTRE DAME: PATERFAMILIAS, POLITICIAN, ENTREPRENEUR

University historian Thomas Schlereth in his book *The University of Notre Dame: A Portrait of Its History and Campus* writes that in the winter of 1842 a a young priest by the name of Edward Sorin set out on a strenuous 250-mile journey northward from his mission station near Vincennes in southern Indiana.[1] Accompanied by six religious brothers, Sorin was on his way to take possession of land in northern Indiana that he had been given tentative title to by the Bishop of Vincennes.[2] The land grant made possible the fulfillment of his dream to establish a Catholic university in the American midwest.

Schlereth describes Sorin's elation upon reaching the site of the future university in the late afternoon of November 26. Sorin was deeply moved by the resplendent placidity of what was known as Ste-Marie-des-Lacs (St. Marie of the Lakes). Writing home to his religious community in France, Sorin described the terrain: ''Everything was frozen and yet the landscape appeared so beautiful. The lake, with its mantle of resplendent white snow, was to us a symbol of the purity of Our Lady, whose name it bears and also of the

15

purity of soul which should characterize the new inhabitants of these lovely shores." Sorin immediately renamed it Notre Dame du Lac, or Our Lady of the Lake.

The 28-year-old Sorin, son of a middle-class farmer in the province of La Mayenne in Brittany, was a member of a newly established French religious community known as the Congregatio a Sancta Cruce, or the Congregation of the Holy Cross. He had originally been a diocesan parish priest in a small French village, but feeling repressed by the parochial atmosphere he joined the new order in the hope that his talents would find fruition. He was not disappointed; for a year after joining the community in 1840, he was sent to southern Indiana.

Schlereth writes that on the rechristened land Sorin found only a primitive log cabin chapel, an Indian interpreter's clapboard house, and a small shed for storing logs. The log chapel had been built ten years earlier by another French priest, Stephen Badin, who was the first priest ordained in the United States. After receiving Holy Orders from Baltimore's Bishop John Carroll in 1783, Badin spent six decades as a missionary in the Mississippi and Ohio Valleys.

Using the Badin chapel as their living quarters, Sorin and his colleagues immediately started cutting down trees to build another log cabin structure nearby. Other buildings followed including the "Old College" which was an all-purpose structure containing classrooms, dormitory, dining hall, and kitchen. This building, whose original structure still exists today, was the university until the main building was built in 1844.

Originally, there were no entrance requirements and students were placed wherever it was thought they would fit into the curriculum. Before studying on the collegiate level, most of the students needed extensive preparatory or remedial work because few had any common-school education and many of their backgrounds were so varied. The rigorous academic regimen, based on French scholastic norms, kept the students occupied from 5:30 a.m. to 6:00 p.m. with classes, study halls, meals, and exercise periods. Students were not allowed to leave the campus except for afternoon walks on Wednesdays and Sundays. Both students and professors arrived and departed at irregular times during the academic year.

In assessing Notre Dame's early years, historian John Wack noted the university's somewhat impoverished beginnings: "A properly charted, substantially constructed, modestly successful seat of learning—inadequately endowed in faculty, students and funds, but at least minimally endowed in all of these, not bankrupt, not intellectually destitute, not unattended, not without hope."[3]

How did such an "inadequately endowed" university survive during the economic, social, and political upheavals of the Civil War era? (Only seven of the 51 Catholic colleges which had been established by 1861 are still in existence. In addition, it has been estimated that 80 percent of the antebellum secular colleges did not survive.)[4] Schlereth believes that a fortunate combination of geography, immigration, philanthropy, and legerdemain account for Notre Dame's thriving survival:

> From Europe came men, money, and Catholic immigrants with sons requiring education; likewise from America came philanthropy in land and cash grants and in the dedicated lives of faculty and staff. The college's position in time and place was also fortuitous: Notre Dame was founded just as the Midwest was opened by canals and railroads; for most of the 1840's Notre Dame was the only Catholic college of consequence with access to such cities as Toledo, Cleveland, Detroit, Milwaukee, and particularly, the rapid-growing city of Chicago. The college's geographic proximity to South Bend, a community soon to be a center of agriculture and industry, aided its growth.[6]

These adventitious circumstances were then appropriated by Sorin, who parlayed fortune and a sparse endowment into the makings of a great university. It was Sorin's informing vision and personality that forged Notre Dame more than that of anyone else.

Sorin's fortitude is best seen in his response to the 1879 fire which destroyed the Main Building, the six-story structure which was in essence the entire university. Returning from a trip to Montreal, Sorin walked immediately to the charred ruins, resolutely circled the remains, and summoned students and faculty into the church. There he addressed the entire university community, concluding with a tenacious observation: "If it were *all* gone, I should not give up."[7] True to his word, the university was rebuilt and continued to grow under Sorin's handpicked successors, young vigorous priests such as Auguste Lemonnier and Thomas Walsh, men possessing both intellectual erudition and financial acumen.

When Sorin died in 1893 he had "parlayed the 524 acres, $300, and a line of limited credit that Bishop Hailandiere had given him in 1842 into an extensive portfolio of landholdings and investments so complex that it took eighteen years to finally settle his estate."[8]

After Sorin's death Notre Dame continued to grow. But it remained fairly anonymous as an institution until the son of a Norwegian immigrant arrived on campus. Knute Kenneth Rockne came to Notre Dame from the northside of Chicago in 1910 to study chemistry. He had saved money for his tuition by working for the U. S. Post Office. He put Notre Dame on the front page of the nation's newspapers by helping to invent football's forward pass with his classmate Gus Dorais and then using the innovation to beat Army in 1914. The public could not believe that such an unheralded school could beat the powerful West Point team.

Graduating magna cum laude in chemistry, Rockne remained at the university to teach chemistry and become assistant football coach.[9] In 1918 he was appointed athletic director and head coach, beginning a career that has never been equaled in the history of football and that has become the substance of legend and myth. From 1918 until 1931 when he died in a Kansas plane crash at the age of 43, Rockne produced football teams of such prowess that sportswriters were forced to use mythological images to describe their grace and beauty. Perhaps the most well-known was that of

Grantland Rice, then the nation's premiere sportswriter, who wrote about Notre Dame defeating Army 13-7 in 1924:

> Outlined against the blue-gray October sky, the Four Horsemen rode again. In dramatic lore they are known as Famine, Pestilence, Destruction, and Death. These are only aliases. Their real names are Stuhldreher, Miller, Crowley, and Layden. They formed the crest of the cyclone before which another fighting Army football team was swept over the precipice of the Polo Grounds yesterday afternoon.[10]

Rockne won 105 games, lost 12, and tied five; five of his teams were undefeated; six lost only one game; and two teams were national champions.

Similar to Bobby Jones, another sports idol of the 1920's, Rockne became a near-mythical folk hero who seemed to transcend the boundaries of the sport in which he excelled. Both Jones and Rockne possessed extraordinarily keen minds and they put that intellectual acumen to work in their chosen field of sport. Little known is the fact that Jones, after earning a degree in mechanical engineering in just three years from Georgia Tech, went to Harvard and received a degree in English literature in three semesters. Two years later in 1926 he entered the Emory University Law School in Atlanta and withdrew after three semesters in order to pass the bar. Rockne himself had a brilliant scientific mind and had he concentrated his intellectual energies in that direction, he could have made, it is said, an original contribution to the sciences,—the kind that was already being made at Notre Dame by Father Julius Nieuwland, who discovered synthetic rubber in 1926.

In addition to the Four Horsemen, Rockne produced a football player who also became a mythical American hero. George Gipp was the consummate athlete who could do anything on the football field—run, pass, kick, and think his way out of the most inextricable entanglements. Rockne had seen Gipp, who had come to Notre Dame on a baseball scholarship, drop-kicking on a practice field.

He invited him to try out for the team and from 1917 to 1920 Gipp enchanted the country with his skills. Ring Lardner wrote of him, "Notre Dame has one signal: Pass the ball to Gipp and let him use his own judgment."[11]

Gipp became Notre Dame's first All-American football player leading the team in rushing, passing and scoring for three years. Shortly after the last game of his career in 1920, Gipp contracted strepthroat and died that December. He was 25 and on his deathbed was said to have made a last request of Rockne. Rockne never revealed what Gipp had asked of him until 1928, when Notre Dame, which had had a poor season losing four games, faced a powerful Army team which was undefeated. In the locker room Rockne told his players, "Before George Gipp died, he said to me, 'Rock, some day when the going is real tough, ask the boys to go out and beat Army for me.' " Notre Dame did exactly that, beating Army 12-6 and the phrase "Win one for the Gipper" became a part of American folklore; for he was the prototypical gifted youth in whom everyone perceived a little of their lost dreams.

While Rockne proved his genius for football, another inventive mind was at work in the Notre Dame chemistry department. In a famous paper read at a 1926 organic chemistry symposium in Rochester, New York, Father Julius Nieuwland (who was Rockne's mentor as a student) revealed his catalytic polymerization of acetylene which resulted in the manufacture of synthetic rubber (neoprene). The polymerization was patented and E.I. du Point de Nemours and Company subsidized further research by Nieuwland, paying him consulting fees and patent royalties. (Interestingly enough, the European-born Nieuwland had not started out in chemistry but first taught botany at the university, founding and editing a bi-monthly scholarly journal, *The American Midland Naturalist.)*

In 1934 Notre Dame gained another of its strong executives in Father John O'Hara, who guided the university through the depression years, becoming a cardinal and the Archbishop of Philadelphia in 1940. A conservative prelate conscious of his image, O'Hara once banned *Time* magazine from campus after it had published a photograph of him in his bathing trunks. He exercised the powers of his office with the filial concern of a pastor of an immigrant Chicago parish. For example, according to *Time* he issued religious bulletins correlating the relationship between a half century of football scores and communion receptions, logging the number of daily genuflections ("448 in Sorin chapel on Tuesday"), and warning students they would be subject to a personal interview if they did not make their Easter duty.

Notre Dame survived the war years through the shrewdness of O'Hara's successor, Father Hugh "Pepper" O'Donnell, who, anticipating the drain of students during a declared war, offered the university's facilities to the army and navy. Two months before President Roosevelt declared war on Japan the navy established a Naval Reserve Officers Training Corps program on the campus. Created by the navy during the war, it was the first of several officer training programs that included Marines. Nearly 12,000 men completed officer training at Notre Dame between 1942 and 1946.[12]

(This tradition of officer training and education continues today at Notre Dame. In 1980, Hesburgh received the Sylvanus Thayer Award from the West Point Corps of Cadets. In his address to the cadets, Hesburgh affirmed the valued presence of officer training programs on the nation's campuses as well as in its service academies. "If the United States wanted automatons for officers, there would be no need to prepare them at honorable places like Notre Dame and West Point," he said.)

In 1941 the university hired Frank Leahy as its football coach. He had played center and left tackle under Rockne himself and was as Irish and Catholic as Rockne was Norwegian and Lutheran (in 1925 Rockne converted to Catholicism). An intense man driven by an insatiable desire for perfection, Leahy firmly believed that he had been predestined to inherit Rockne's legacy.[13] His teams were near models of athletic perfection with players (whom Leahy affectionately referred to as "my lads") of such consummate skill that four of them, Angelo Bertelli (1943), Johnny Lujack (1947), Leon Hart (1949), and Johnny Lattner (1953) won the Heisman Trophy. Six of Leahy's teams were undefeated and four won national championships.

Leahy could inspire and chastise with equal fervor, driving his players and himself beyond their limits. He delivered locker room orations in sonorous tones and with a mist in his eyes that was at once both ingenuous and guileful.

Leahy's predilection for perfection extended to every detail imaginable. He hired a force of security guards to patrol the second floors of buildings which overlooked the practice field in order to prevent spying from the opposition. It was reported that Leahy even chartered an airplane to patrol the area surrounding the practice field to ferret out clandestine agents from other teams who could be hiding in trees.

In a famous game against Iowa in 1953, Leahy instructed a player to feign an injury near the end of the first half when Notre Dame had no time-outs left. When the player did, Notre Dame gained enough time to score and eventually secure a tie. Such tactics indicated that Leahy was both physically and emotionally enervated. "Coaching burns out a man's insides. It's more than tension. Oh, it was far worse," Leahy conceded.[14] At the end of the 1953 season, Leahy resigned for reasons of health.

Also, the emigration of refugee scholars driven from Europe by the Nazis continued. University of Chicago historian John Nef described the arrival of these intellectual emigrés as "the Notre Dame Renaissance."[15] One such emigré was Waldemar Gurian, a political scientist and historian. A Russian Jew converted to Catholicism, Gurian founded the Review of Politics at Notre Dame. He became, along with his friend Hannah Arendt, one of the foremost observers of totalitarianism, examining its spurious assumptions with a philosopher's rigor.

In her book *Men in Dark Times* Hanna Arendt wrote a series of essays on selected men and women whom she believed illumined their age with a particular lucidity by virtue of the wholeness of their life and thought. Arendt wrote that Gurian possessed a sympathy extending not only to the company of those he knew and loved, but embraced a larger realm—the impoverished and oppressed.

The groundwork for the emergence of Notre Dame as a great modern university was laid by Hesburgh's predecessor, Father John J. Cavanaugh, a strong priest-executive in the tradition of Sorin and Hesburgh, combining financial dexterity and wide-ranging intellectual interests. Before becoming a priest, Cavanaugh garnered considerable experience in the business world. In fact, he worked as a secretary in the office of Henry Ford before entering Notre Dame where he received a business degree in 1923. He then went to work for Studebaker in South Bend as an advertising manager. Resigning to enter the seminary, Cavanaugh earned a master's degree in English literature and then received an advanced degree in philosophy at the Gregorian University in Rome. He succeeded O'Donnell as president in 1946 and used his business acumen to set up a foundation to raise $25 million and begin a permanent university endowment.

Cavanaugh possessed an intellectual vision and frequently asked an impassioned query: "Where are the Catholic Salks, Oppenheimers, Einsteins?"[16] To foster such an intellectual tradition Cavanaugh set up an institute of Medieval Studies, a natural law institute, a research group of scholars known as the Committee on International Relations, and a pioneering germ-free laboratory known as LOBUND (Laboratories of Bacteriology at the University of Notre Dame). He also reorganized the university administration, placing a young theology teacher, Theodore Hesburgh, then just 32, in the position of executive vice-president (Cavanaugh once said of Hesburgh, "You'd have to be blind not to spot his talents.").

Hesburgh's 35-year tenure has brought many dramatic changes to the university. Enrollment has risen from 4,979 to 9,676 (undergraduate and graduate) and the faculty from 389 to 951. The university's endowment has increased from $9 million to $350 million, ranking it 18th in the country.

The university's annual operating budget increased from $9.7 million to $176.6 million and its research funding from $735,000 to $15 million. The replacement value of the physical plant increased from $24 million in 1951-52 to $492 million today. Forty buildings were built during Hesburgh's tenure including a 13-story library, several residence halls, a new faculty building, a center for continuing education, a building for computer sciences, several new germ-free laboratories, an addition to the law school, an athletic and convocation center, and a new engineering building.

The library has grown from 338,000 volumes to 1.6 million, with space for a million more books. Annual giving has grown from $1.1 million to $48.3 million with 86 percent of the alumni participating.

Hesburgh did not accomplish this alone. Essential to Hesburgh's success in transforming Notre Dame into one of the nation's best universities was Rev. Edmund P. Joyce, Hesburgh's partner for 35 years as executive vice president.

Joyce's financial, accounting and administrative skills guided the accelerated growth in the university's endowment, faculty salaries, and physical plant (now worth $492 million). Under Joyce and Hesburgh, faculty salaries increased from $5,000 to $47,485 per year, one of the highest median levels in the nation. Joyce also administered the university athletic program.

Frank Meier, Chicago Bureau Chief for *Newsweek,* reported in *Notre Dame Magazine* (Winter 1987) that Joyce was instrumental in organizing the university's development and fund-raising efforts. "His major role in the planning and execution of the Ford Foundation's challenge grants and the creation of the University's fund-raising apparatus are largely unknown to the Notre Dame family," Meier wrote.

Joyce preferred to remain in the background quietly wielding immense influence in university decision-making. Born in Spartanburg, South Carolina, in 1917, Joyce came to Notre Dame at the urging of a local pastor. He graduated *magna cum laude* in 1938 with a B. S. in accounting.

According to Meier, when Joyce returned to Spartanburg and joined an accounting firm, he took an active interest in the Church as a Catholic layman often debating back country evangelists on Sundays. Hearing a call to the priesthood, Joyce entered Holy Cross Seminary in 1942 and was ordained in 1949.

The university sent Joyce to Oxford for study in philosophy, politics and economics. Upon his return to Notre Dame, Joyce was soon named executive vice president beginning a unique 35-year partnership with its new president Theodore Hesburgh.

Hesburgh described their relationship to Meier: "Ned (Joyce) and I are different in so many ways you wouldn't think we'd make a good team. He's a Southerner, I'm a Yankee. He's quite conservative, I'm quite liberal. He's good with numbers, I'm better with words. He knows how to raise money, I'm better at spending it. . .Everything I lack, he seems to have," says Hesburgh.

In 1967, Hesburgh moved to have the university governed by a lay board of trustees rather than by priests of his congregation. He believed it would augment intellectual freedom on campus and help recruit the best teachers.

In another dramatic move, women were admitted to the university for the first time in 1972. That change made the Notre Dame community feel more like a "family" Hesburgh told the student newspaper *The Observer* in October 1986.

All in all, Hesburgh's term as chancellor of Notre Dame meets full circle with that of its originator, Father Sorin. The similarities between the two are uncanny, not just as priest-entrepreneurs, but in other ways as well.

Sorin loved children with the indulgence of a grandfather and, Schlereth writes, "he was not above lugging a bushel of peaches" to the primary school, playing with children in residence on the campus, or even "shooting marbles with them in their dirt play yard."[17]

At the home of his brother in Pacific Palisades, California, Hesburgh gave each of his six nieces and nephews special care and attention, tumbling the smaller ones in the air after dinner as well as helping with the washing and drying of the dinner dishes. Vernon Jordan, former director of the National Urban League who served with Hesburgh on the Clemency Board, says that "when he calls my home he always spends a lot of time talking to my teenage daughter. This, to me, is typical of the interest he takes in young people. He always has time for them."

Father Wilson has observed Hesburgh's concern for the young at close range and says: "Even as president, he always found time for his younger brother, his nephews and nieces when they were in attendance at Notre Dame. He would visit their rooms and take the opportunity for 'rap' sessions with students in nearby rooms. He is available day or night to say Mass for a student who has died or been injured in an auto accident. Many foreign students have been recipients of his time and care. One family of students, five girls and their brother, certainly were the objects of his loving concern for quite a few years. They took all their problems to him. He had a very special interest in the Notre Dame students working in the Peace Corp and other government programs and if his travels took him anywhere these students were working, he would make the time to visit them.

"My office was located near Father Ted's," he continues "and in the evening many students would walk up to the third floor of the Administration Building to talk with him. They might want to talk with him about academics, student affairs, or personal problems. He always had time to help a student with personal problems and if his schedule was too busy, he would always get another priest or faculty member to help and advise the student."

Sorin was a tenacious negotiator who drove hard bargains. Schlereth writes that "in business transactions he could exhibit all the traits the French have in mind by the term *sangfroid.*" For example, Sorin secured title to 185 acres of farm property along St. Mary's Creek, a stream draining one of the university's two lakes (St. Mary's and St. Joseph's Lakes). Sorin had repeatedly tried to buy the property for commercial investment and expansion purposes. In addition, he believed that the high water level of the lake itself and the stagnant marsh lying between the two lakes had caused the malaria and cholera which had killed 23 priests, brothers, sisters, and students by 1855.[19] If he could gain title to the property to control the creek, the lake's water level could be lowered and the marsh dried by draining them through the creek's dam. When the malarial fever and cholera once again reached epidemic proportions, Sorin approached the land's owner, a man named Rush, and this time found him amenable to the sale. Schlereth narrates what happened:

> The initial papers were drawn up, but Rush suddenly left town without signing them. Sorin, not a man accustomed to be kept waiting, felt a decision had been agreed upon in the spirit if not the letter of the law. Without hesitation he dispatched six burly workmen to destroy Rush's dam while he went off to celebrate the Holy Thursday Eucharist in memory of those who had died during the epidemic. Rush, upon his return, accepted the *fait accompli* and closed the sale for $8,000 as originally arranged. The university was expanded . . . the lake level sank, the marsh dried, and the cholera vanished.

Hesburgh also is a negotiator of formidable stature.[20] Dr. Stephen Horn, vice chairman of the Civil Rights Commission and president of California State University, Long Beach, says that Daniel Patrick Moynihan, who served along with Leonard Garment as President Nixon's principal liaison with the commission, once told him that Hesburgh was "the toughest person he ever had to deal with." Horn explains "that this is based on the fact that he'll look at you and smile, knowing all the time where he wants to go. He's a tough bargainer having pretty much figured out all the nuances before he starts negotiating. His mind works very rapidly while he's bargaining with his eye right on the goal. He might compromise with you a little bit on the tactics along the way, but he knows what he wants and he has the good will and determination to get exactly that. I think he's a very pragmatic person. Yet his idealism has never been compromised.

The formidable nature of Hesburgh's negotiating and bargaining powers can be seen in his dealings not only with the Nixon Administration over Civil Rights but also in direct confrontations with such powerful military figures as Chilean dictator Augusto Pinochet and the Marine Corps commander in Vietnam, General Lewis Walt. Shortly after the 1973 military coup which deposed Chilean President Salvador Allende Gossens and resulted in his death, Hesburgh heard that General Pinochet, the head of the military junta who had installed himself as chief of state, had been threatening to expropriate St. George's College, the parochial high school in Santiago owned and administered by the Congregation of the Holy Cross, the religious order to which Hesburgh belongs. Hesburgh flew to Santiago and in a private meeting with the dictator told him in no uncertain terms what the consequences of such an action would be; he would make sure that the general's position with regard to the Catholic Church worldwide as well as in Chile would not merely be uncomfortable, but in a word untenable. Pinochet backed down and no action was taken against the school.

As a member of the Clemency Board, a role which will be discussed in detail later, Hesburgh and General Walt confronted each other with their diametrically opposed views on clemency and engaged in a series of impassioned debates in which Hesburgh emerged as the board's conscience.

Sorin was a master politician whose tact and diplomacy enabled him to cast virtual spells over anyone he came in contact with. "*Savoir faire* with adults was also a Sorin forte," Schlereth writes.[21] "He could charm a faculty member into staying on another year despite a proffered meager salary, play social lion to the South Bend gentry with private dinner parties *á la Parisien,* and keep good press relations with an annual New Year's Day gift to the local newspaper's staff."[22] (Often the gift would be a vintage French wine or liqueur.)

Hesburgh, too, is the supreme politician and diplomat. "Father Ted is the ablest politician I've ever known, and I say that in the highest sense of the word, in the Aristotelian sense that there is no higher calling than politics or serving one's own society," says Civil Rights Vice Chairman Dr. Stephen Horn, himself an educator not unfamiliar with politicians.

This observation is reflected in the comments of Clemency Board Associate General Counsel John Foote who says, "The essence of Hesburgh's politics is a deeply-felt humanism. It is the most remarkable humanistic approach I have ever witnessed." Civil Rights Commissioner Manuel Ruiz, Jr. observes, "He is very inspirational and very committed. He doesn't care if you particularly agree with him or not but that does not mean he is not diplomatic." An example of Hesburgh uniting politics and diplomacy is recalled by Howard Glickstein, former Staff Director of the Civil Rights Commission. "The Commission always had trouble getting funds from Congress every year. The Chairman of the House committee which had to approve our appropriation was the late Congressman John Rooney of Brooklyn. The only two people he ever treated with any respect were J. Edgar Hoover and Father Hesburgh. When Father Hesburgh would appear before Rooney's committee, Rooney would never ask a word about the budget. He would just ask Father Hesburgh when was the last time he had seen the Pope. Then they would exchange priest stories with each other, both of them using a thick Irish accent."

At social gatherings Hesburgh moved among guests with the consummate ease of a career diplomat, stopping to talk with nearly everyone, calling some aside for a private conversation, leaving a group so gracefully when he felt he should move that there was no impression that he had left abruptly.

What Schlereth writes of Sorin can also be said of Hesburgh: "He was part confidence man, part visionary, part paterfamilias."

CHAPTER 4
HESBURGH AND NOTRE DAME:
THE IDEA OF A UNIVERSITY

In June of 1952 Cavanaugh appointed Hesburgh president of the university upon the expiration of his six-year term that month. Upon assuming office, the 35-year-old Hesburgh immediately began moving the university toward more rigorous academic standards. "I would rather see Notre Dame die than be educationally mediocre. We will be the best, or please God, we will cease to exist here," he declared. He thereby restricted undergraduate enrollment to 5,500; today it is 7,552, raised admission standards by requiring higher scores on the Scholastic Aptitude Tests, increased the graduate enrollment, restructured the curriculum in liberal arts, business, law, engineering, and discarded scores of vocational courses. But beyond this concerted drive for the highest intellectual achievement, Hesburgh had something even more audacious in mind. Hesburgh was attempting to create a university commensurate with the vision of John Henry Cardinal Newman, the great priest-intellectual of 19th century English Catholicism. In *The Idea of a University*, Newman had envisioned the university as a locus for exploration and teaching knowledge as a universal or organic whole. "That only is the true enlargement of the mind which is the power

Theodore Hesburgh with mother and sisters.

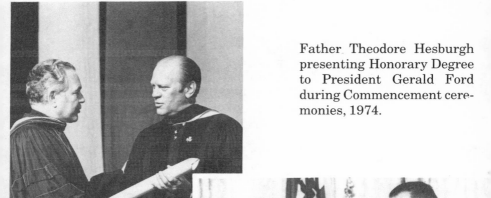

Father Theodore Hesburgh presenting Honorary Degree to President Gerald Ford during Commencement ceremonies, 1974.

President Johnson shakes hands with Father Theodore Hesburgh after presenting him with a Presidential Freedom Medal in a ceremony at the White House, 1964.

Father Hesburgh and President Carter in White House, 1979

President Kennedy and Father Hesburgh look at the Laetare Medal presented to the Chief Executive November 22, 1961 at the White House.

President Eisenhower hands out commissions to the civil rights commission.

With President Ronald Reagan at Commencement ceremonies, 1981.

Pope John XXIII with Father Hesburgh and Mr. Folsom of RCA.

Father Hesburgh with Pope Pius XII, 1956.

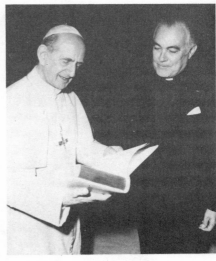

Pope Pius VI with Theodore Hesburgh, 1977.

With Pope John Paul II at a recent meeting of the Pontifical Council for Culture in Rome. Father Hesburgh is the American member of the 14-person group formed in 1982.

Father Hesburgh being sworn in by Tip O'Neil for the Commission on Holocaust at the White House.

Martin Luther King, Sr. and Father Hesburgh at Sacred Heart Church.

Commencement 1979 Helen Hayes Laetare Medal award.

Ambassador Robert Murphy congratulates Hesburgh on receiving the NCCJ's Charles Evans Hughes Award in New York.

At interview with Author Ellie Weisel.

Napoleon Duarte with Hesburgh during his visit to Notre Dame for Commencement, 1985.

On the U.S. Civil Rights Commission.

Yale President Kingman Brewster Jr. and Darek Bok, Harvard President-elect, in 1971.

During a Mass on Notre Dame's Antihunger Day, Father Hesburgh urges action to end hunger.

Walking with students on campus.

of viewing many things at once," he wrote. "All knowledge forms one thing," he continued, "because its subject-matter is one, for the universe in its length and breadth is so intimately knit together, that we cannot separate off portion from portion, and operation from operation, except by a mental abstraction."

Another 19th century thinker, an American historian named Henry Adams, had anticipated the twentieth century's response to such a theological posture toward knowing and, after attempting it himself, disparaged the endeavor as inherently self-destructive. Declaring that historians had got themselves into too much trouble by using theological models to augment their synthesis, he wrote with finality that, "For human purposes a point must always be soon reached where larger synthesis is suicide." Hesburgh, however, unwilling to conform to such an epistemology or escape from its consequences, believes with the same intellectual ardor as Newman that there should be an informing vision in the pursuit of knowledge and that knowledge—despite its disparate character—does possess a centrality, an integral unity reflecting the transcendent nature of reality. It is not by chance, for example, that the contemporary philosophic mind which has probably influenced Hesburgh more than any other is that of the late French philosopher Jacques Maritain. One would think that Hesburgh has recently been in the company of Maritain, Newman, or one of the great medieval Christian philosophic synthesizers when he discusses the role of the Catholic university in a secular age. "In the whole spectrum of kinds of universities," Hesburgh stated, "the Catholic university is that which does its university task of seeking truth and proclaiming truth with an openness to the order of transcendence which most universities don't do in the secular order. The Catholic university possesses an added dimension in the notion that there is a completeness and oneness in the order of knowing."

Philosophy and theology, which Hesburgh calls "the sciences of transcendence" are integral to this openness. "They are the sciences that get beyond the immediate, the practical, the here and now—to what is ultimately of infinite value and virtue," he explains. These were the very disciplines which prepared Hesburgh for specialized tasks and projects, which are usually given only to "experts" and "professionals."

"I had a very liberal education—not only liberal in the conventional sense but on the upper end of liberal—majoring in philosophy in college and theology in graduate school," Hesburgh says. "You could say that it would prepare you for just about nothing except maybe being a priest. Yet I started out as a counselor in a reform school. Then I did work in a parish that involved a lot of things other than theology such as running a USO club during World War II. I was a chaplain in the service for a while and later a chaplain for the married students at Notre Dame. That involved all kinds of things— making marriage successful, housing, and recreation.

"Then I got into administration and was in charge of the university's building program raising $19 million. I was appointed a member of the National Science Board and since I had no background in science, I had to learn that on my own. As a result, I became involved in research programs in Antarctica, space, and high energy physics. Through the Civil Rights movement I became acquainted with law. For 15 years in Vienna I attended the annual conferences of the International Atomic Energy Agency and worked on the peaceful uses of atomic energy. I helped reform the Naval Academy, instituting an educational program at one point and becoming chairman of the Board of Visitors at Annapolis. Once I even reviewed and checked aviation training for the Navy."

As an administrator and leader, Hesburgh acts decisively, believes in delegation, manages his time with precision and flexibility, and espouses a humane philosophy of management. These qualities enabled him to lead the university with an informing vision— although not always without conflict and challenge.

The student disruptions of the late 1960's and early 1970's directly challenged Hesburgh's authority and leadership. The attempt by the Teamsters Union in the late 1970's to unionize university service workers beginning with the groundskeepers also challenged Hesburgh's moral and institutional authority.

In 1978, the Teamsters Union began an active campaign on campus to organize the university's groundskeepers. The university objected on the grounds that the groundskeepers were an inappropriate bargaining unit and appealed to the National Labor Relations Board. The NLRB agreed, ruling that the groundskeepers possessed no unique skills, training, pay rates or jobs to qualify as a unit distinct from other workers at the university.

In effect, the university did not want the Teamsters on campus. The university's director of personnel told the *South Bend Tribune,* "If employee needs are met, I don't think a union is needed. We can meet the same needs and probably meet them better without a union presence."

The director also said that the university did not want the Teamsters because of its alleged relationship with organized crime and its approach to bargaining and power.

Nevertheless, Hesburgh and the university were criticized by students and labor advocacy groups for their position. The *South Bend Tribune* reported on January 16, 1979: "The groundkeepers' issue raised considerable reaction among the students and nationally, particularly because of Rev. Theodore M. Hesburgh's role in civil rights, and the Catholic Church's teachings unionization of workers. Students also apparently took an interest because of the high number of Chicanos included in the groundkeeping force."

In managing university affairs, Hesburgh structured the university administration so that there were only two university officers directly reporting to him: the executive vice president and the provost.

This division of responsibility was efficient in that it separated academic affairs from financial administration. The executive vice president was responsible for finances, buildings and grounds, university relations and athletics. The provost had responsibility for academic and student affairs.

Once a month, Hesburgh would call the executive vice president, provost, other vice presidents and their key advisors for a meeting.

As Hesburgh explains in *What Works for Me*, a collection of essays on management style of 16 chief executive officers: "Anyone can put anything they want on the agenda. In this way I am not constantly having a stream of vice presidents running in and out. I see the provost and the executive vice president almost every day and the other vice presidents are free to see me any time; but they know they'd better not be coming to me about something they haven't talked over with their own vice president first."[1]

Such structuring allowed Hesburgh to adopt a policy of almost total accessibility to students, faculty members and alumni. Hesburgh said that some might think this would be "ruinous."[2] However, Hesburgh found that people did not abuse his accessibility. In fact, he found these contacts to be a renewing resource which kept him from being isolated from external influences.[3]

The art of delegation is another salient quality of Hesburgh's management style. Hesburgh believes delegation is one of the keys to management: "It's my rule never, never to do anyone else's job. If I hear something startling, I may put a little note on it, but I never make the decision for them."[4]

Despite his philosophy of in-depth delegation, Hesburgh also believes in hands-on management when the consequences are far-reaching. One example is the selection of faculty members for tenure. "You have to know when to do hands-on, and obviously it's hands-on when people's lives are involved," he explained.[5] Hesburgh read every tenure candidate's folder thoroughly before making the final decision (13 persons, including the provost, college deans and department heads make judgments before the folder reaches Hesburgh's desk).

In *What Works for Me*, Hesburgh estimated that in 35 years as president of Notre Dame he has spent 45 years working part time on commissions and major task forces and more than that on boards of private organizations (he estimates he spent ten years as Chairman of the Overseas Development Council, 21 years on the Rockefeller Foundation Board and six years as its chairman, and seven years on the Chase Manhattan Board).[6]

The extent of Hesburgh's involvement in and outside the university requires managing multiple responsibilities. "I've never held just one job but rather about five concurrently," he said. "But I pay attention only to what I am doing right now. I manage to be able to focus only on what I am doing, and then when that is over, I'll take up the next thing."

"This means reading the minutes of the last meeting, in preparation for the next one, on the airplane, carrying in my briefcase (more of a Gladstone bag) four or five fairly thick folders. When I read this material just before a meeting I am freshly briefed on it."[7]

Hesburgh's philosophy of leadership as a university president is found in the words of a well-known Renaissance figure, the Duke of Mantua. The Duke described the art of governing simply as *essere umano*, to be human.[8] Hesburgh quoted these words in an address "The University President" he gave to the American Council of Education in 1976. Hesburgh explained that there was a humane way of saying no, of denying a request, or telling someone they have failed. "There is a humane way of upholding a deeply held conviction, even when it is under brutal attack. One can be forceful and humane at the same time. But it is not easy," he told the educators.

Hesburgh is guided by the principle that management and decision-making involve a moral dimension as well. It is not that every decision is a moral crisis but that to ignore the moral element in a decision poses a considerable risk—especially for the virtue of justice.[9]

Justice is a primary concern for Hesburgh. He believes that the Christian university is worthless unless it instills a profound sense of the dignity of the human person and the opportunities for seeking justice in an unjust world. "One does not need a suit of armor, or a white horse, or a sword, but just a sensitivity to justice wherever it is endangered, a quiet passion to be concerned for justice in our times, a compassion for all men who suffer injustice, or the fruits of injustice."[10]

Hesburgh is a firm advocate of liberal education and looks with some alarm on the current trend toward vocational training in American education. He often refers to the generous predisposition of the mind described by Newman as the natural consequence of a liberal education. "A habit of mind is formed," Newman wrote, "which lasts through life, of which the attributes are freedom, equitableness, calmness, moderation, and wisdom; or what in a former Discourse I have ventured to call a philosophical habit." Hesburgh does not deny the necessary and practical value of education for a vocation but he believes vocation alone is not enough to make life finally rewarding.

"You certainly have to learn how to be an accountant, a businessman, a doctor, lawyer, a priest, or a teacher," he concedes. "But everyone should, I think, have some liberal education. If all I learn is how to do one thing—to put this screw in this wheel in this automobile—then that means for the rest of my life I'm going to be doing just that. It seems to me that is a terrible prospect for any human being.

"Liberal education is the kind of education where we get our values. It is the kind of education from which we derive the great treasures of human philosophical wisdom, and scientific discovery. It is the education that enables us to think the long thoughts concerning the meaning of existence, life and death, war and peace, love and hate, the meaning of the family. It is the education that gives meaning to your individual existence because you can learn how to situate yourself in life as a man or a woman, young or old, American Indian, Black or White, Protestant, Catholic, Jewish, or non-believer. You come to understand your human situation and discover how to cherish it and grow in it."

According to Schlereth, distinguished lecturers (e.g. Arnold Toynbee, Martin D'Arcy, Jacques Maritain) were invited to campus and superior scholars were hired as permanent faculty to increase the school's academic standing.[11] By the end of Hesburgh's first six-year term in 1958, academic development was well on its way. In addition, both faculty and students were more intellectually mature.

One indication of the growing academic excellence was that 18 undergraduates were named to Woodrow Wilson Teaching Fellowships, ranking Notre Dame fifth in the nation. In the summer of 1958, the Congregation of Holy Cross separated Hesburgh's role as superior of the order from the presidency. Since the superior's term was for six years, this allowed him to be president with no definite term of office.

More evidence of improved academic performance came in 1960 when the Ford Foundation awarded Notre Dame a matching grant of $6 million if the university could rase $12 million within a three-year period.[12] The Ford Foundation also offered similar grants to five other improving universities: Johns Hopkins, Vanderbilt, University of Denver, Brown and Stanford. The fund-raising campaign was known as Challenge I and it raised money for faculty development, student aid and scholarships, a Freshman Year of Studies program, and area studies in Latin America, East Europe and Africa. Challenge I also financed several new facilities including the Computing Center and Mathematics Building (1962) and the 14-story Memorial Library (1963).

Challenge II (1963-66) raised $18 million and provided financing for the Athletic and Convocation Center (1968).[13] The SUMMA campaign (1967-72) raised $62 million to endow distinguished professorships, improve graduate education, fund minority scholarships and student loans, and launch special projects such as the Institute for Advanced Religious Studies.[14]

In the early 1960's, students began to challenge Hesburgh's authority. Demonstrations occurred to end dormitory regulations. A 1961 student report-manifesto advocated increased intellectual achievement and excellence. Student editors tried restructuring the university, but bridled under editorial restrictions. According to

Schlereth, Hesburgh countered these criticisms with long epistle-like personal letters to the university community.[15]

Because Hesburgh was frequently absent from the university due to his national and international commitments to public service, Schlereth writes, reforming students and faculty proposed that Hesburgh's executive powers be divided into the separate offices of president and chancellor.[16] No action was taken on this proposal although seven years later the university created the office of university provost. The provost is the university's chief academic officers and the acting president in the absence of the president.

Hesburgh's authority remained intact, however, and his pursuit of excellence continued. Hesburgh believes that the special character of Notre Dame is found in its Catholicity. "I think it would have to be the Catholic character because it is that which gave it birth and that which was the substance of the dedication of so many people for so long. It is that which we are very conscious of today, especially when we see so many private schools going out of business. Those schools which are going to survive will do so because of their unique character, and our unique character is to be a Catholic University. Some people think that is an impossibility—you know George Barnard Shaw said that it is a contradiction in terms but I don't believe that. It is an historical fact that the first universities that were founded—Paris, Oxford, Cambridge, Bologna, Salamanca, Louvain—were all Catholic. Historical events led them to cease being Catholic but that had nothing to do per se with the impossibility of their existence because they did exist and they were great universities."

Hesburgh offers his own vision of Notre Dame. "From that day to this there have not been any great Catholic universities, and we are trying to create one in our time." And Hesburgh has done exactly that, making Notre Dame a pre-eminent Catholic university. Former Yale president Kingman Brewster, Jr. says in his preface to *The Human Imperative*, at the Terry Lectures Hesburgh delivered at Yale in 1974: "He has brought the University of Notre Dame to the first rank of the nation's universities; without betraying the sponsorship of his church and his order."

According to Hesburgh, the role of a Catholic university in a secular world is to provide a locus in which the Church can confront the contemporary world and its problems. "The Catholic University," he explains, "gives the Church a place to think in order to meet the world and its variegated problems. You will remember that Vatican II's Schema 13 on the Church in the modern world outlined a lot of problems but did not give very many answers, the reason being that many of these problems were of a social and economic order and answers to them require the kind of research capability that is almost always found in a university."

This role as Catholic university involves nurturing religious art which Hesburgh has also done. It was Hesburgh who helped bring one of the major figures in 20th century sculpture, Yugoslavian sculptor Ivan Mestrovic, to Notre Dame. In 1915 Mestrovic had been the first living artist to be honored by the Victoria and Albert Museum with a one-man show. His stature continued to grow as he created sculptures suffused with themes of grace and redemption culminating, in his great *Pieta* executed while exiled in Rome during World War II (the Vatican had secured his release from house arrest in occupied Zagreb). The face of the dead Christ is so intensely moving that some critics have said it is one of the few Pietas that can compel the same deep emotion elicited by Michaelangelo's *Pieta* in St. Peter's. In 1946 when the Metropolitan Museum of Art honored Mestrovic with a one-man show, the first living artist so honored in 75 years, he came to live in the United States in Hesburgh's home town, Syracuse, where he taught and had a studio at Syracuse University.

Upon learning of Mestrovic from Father Anthony Lauck, who studied with the artist in 1949 in Syracuse, Hesburgh went to the sculptor's studio on one of his trips home. "I was very much attracted to his work," Hesburgh recalls. "I thought he was the greatest Christian artist of the age. He told me he wanted to spend his last years creating religious art in an environment congenial to his vision. I said 'How about Notre Dame?' and he replied, 'It occurred to me and my wife that Notre Dame would be a place where my work would really be appreciated, as you have on your campus a religious sense.'''

Hesburgh built a studio for him where he worked and taught until his death in 1962. Hesburgh also helped secure the transfer of Mestrovic's Rome *Pieta* from the Metropolitan Museum of Art to Notre Dame, where it now resides in Sacred Heart Church. Hesburgh remembers that when the sculpture arrived from New York it was moved to its resting place by a crew of hardened laborers. "It was the roughest, toughest roust-about crowd that we have at the university. They took the canvas off and these four or five tough fellows just stood there in awe for a good five minutes. And that, I thought, was a great recommendation — its impact on even the unlettered."

Hesburgh also has a deep affinity for music, often listening to the works of Beethoven as he labors in his office late into the evening and early morning. This interest in music led to a long friendship with Richard Tucker, the great Metropolitan Opera tenor. Hesburgh, in fact, delivered an effective tribute to Tucker, who was Jewish, in his eulogy at the memorial mass in St. Patrick's Cathedral.

As he finished, according to a *New York Times* reporter, the singer's widow and one of his sons nodded to each other, obviously moved. "All I can say to you, my friends, is that this great man whom we remember so fondly today was a very unusual person," Hesburgh said. "Perhaps the most private memory of this unusual man was that of his three sons who often heard him chant the Kiddush with the traditional blessings of the bread and wine as their mother lit the sabbath lights. You will hear echoes of these lovely blessings in the offertory prayers of the mass today. It reminds us that mass was first offered at a seder in Jerusalem." Hesburgh concluded by reading the mourners' Kaddish, the Jewish prayer for the dead.

CHAPTER 5
CEASE AND DESIST:
THE STUDENT DISRUPTIONS

In the late 1960's, the "uncommitted" generation of students had suddenly undergone a radical metamorphosis and had become passionately committed to ending what they considered an unjust war in Vietnam, as well as equally unjust treatment of blacks and other minorities at home. In a 1965 study, *The Uncommitted*, Kenneth Keniston, a professor of psychology at the Yale Medical School, had described youth's restless search for identity in an American society which apparently rewarded only competitive success. Unable to find life-models in their own fathers or the nation's leaders, many withdrew into idiosyncratic lifestyles, rejected their families and their families' universities, scorned politics and reveled in their own private alienation. But, as Keniston observed, "private alienations are a luxury that only Utopias can afford." In 1968 the disparity between the visionary promise of the "Great Society" and the rude and traumatic reality of two political assassinations, violent race riots in the streets and a psychologically devastating enemy offensive in South Vietnam was only too evident.

The uncommitted generation of students, unable to find fulfillment in their alienation, rebelled against their fathers' conservative society and their surrogate fathers represented by university faculty, administrators, and presidents. On February 17, 1969, a two-column headline on the front page of the *New York Times* read: "U. of Wisconsin Disrupted: Notre Dame gives warning." Underneath followed two separate stories filed the same day, one from Madison, Wisconsin and the other from South Bend, Indiana. The second paragraph of the story from Madison read:

> About 200 of the guardsmen rushed to the campus from standby stations this morning when demonstrators entered classrooms, blocked traffic on campus and city streets, pulled fire alarms in campus buildings and turned on water hoses in the halls. Water seeped into the classrooms.

The reason for such action by the National Guard was to quell disruptions caused by Wisconsin student strikers demanding a black studies department at the university.

By early 1969 such disturbances were not uncommon throughout the nation, whether it was a protest for a black studies department or against the war in Vietnam. Notre Dame itself had been disrupted in November 1968 when students had obstructed campus access from recruiters from Dow Chemical Company (which was then manufacturing napalm to be used in Vietnam) and the Central Intelligence Agency.

The *Times'* story from South Bend told of a warning issued by the president of the University of Notre Dame which threatened immediate expulsion for anyone disrupting normal campus operations. "Anyone or any group that substitutes force for rational persuasion, be it violent or nonviolent will be given 15 minutes of meditation to cease and desist," Hesburgh wrote in an eight-page open letter to the university community. In clear, emphatic terms he declared that disregard for the law on campus would make the existence of the university untenable:

Without the law, the university is a sitting duck for any small group from outside or inside that wishes to destroy it, to incapacitate it, to terrorize it at whim. The argument goes—or has gone—invoke the law and you lose the university community. My only response is that without the law you may well lose the university—and beyond that—the larger society that supports it and that is most deeply wounded when law is no longer respected, bringing an end of everyone's most cherished rights. . . Somewhere a stand must be made.

Students who would not "cease and desist" after the 15-minute period would be asked for their identity cards. Those with cards would be suspended immediately and given five minutes to cease demonstrating before being expelled from the university. Those without cards would be presumed not to be members of the university community and would be arrested as trespassers. Hesburgh wrote of the futility of force and called from compassion's quietude to appease social conflict and disorder:

The last thing a shaken society needs is more shaking. The last thing a noisy, turbulent, and disintegrating community needs is more noise, turbulence, and disintegration. Understanding and analysis of social ills cannot be conducted in a boiler factory. Compassion has a quiet way of service. Complicated social mechanisms, out-of-joint, are not adjusted with sledge hammers.

In the last paragraph of the letter, Hesburgh warned that the university as an autonomous community questing for truth was in grave jeopardy, so much so that he expressed his own disquieting fear that fascism could easily be reborn unless the university community took steps to protect itself from a disrupting and violent truancy. The letter concluded with a solemn warning: "We rule ourselves, or others rule us, in a way that destroys the university as we have known and loved it."

Confronted by this imminent civil disobedience which would have
severely inhibited if not precluded the university community's
intellectual work, Hesburgh put his own career on the line in his
defense of the university's right to preserve its own autonomy by
disciplining those who would disrupt its academic life:[1]

> I have no intention of presiding over such a spectacle:
> too many people have given too much of themselves and
> their lives to this University to let this happen here.
> Without being melodramatic, if this conviction makes
> this my last will and testament to Notre Dame, so be it . . .

Hesburgh's letter, coming in the midst of rising turmoil on the
nation's campuses, evoked a response not only at Notre Dame, but
nationwide as well. Newspapers printed editorials praising the
Notre Dame president's decision and President Nixon sent Hesburgh a personal letter on February 24 supporting his position:

> I share your concern over the recent disorders that have
> paralyzed campus after campus across our country in
> recent weeks, and I want to applaud the forthright stand
> you have taken...

The reaction from the Notre Dame community, although generally favorable, was marked by some strong dissent. In their appraisal
of Hesburgh's tenure, *Hesburgh's Notre Dame: Triumph in Transition,* Joel Connelly and Howard Dooley noted the three following critical reactions. Robert Sam Anson, then editor of the student
newspaper *The Observer,* later a war correspondent for *Time Magazine,* sent Hesburgh a telegram calling for his resignation:

> Statement on student protestors betrays utter disregard
> for due process. Will succeed only in provoking further
> disruption. For good of all, sadly but strongly suggest
> your immediate resignation.*

Connelly and Dooley report that another alumnus wrote a satirical letter suggesting that Hesburgh's approach regarding dissenters was rather inquisitional and reminiscent of the medieval Church's draconian ostracism of heretics:

> He simply revived the age-old policy of the Catholic Church toward dissent: accusation of heresy (disruption), followed by an opportunity to recant (fifteen-minute meditation) and, should this fail, excommunication (expulsion) and surrender of the sinner to the secular arm (police).

Dr. Franklin Murphy, former chancellor of UCLA, believes Hesburgh's strong stand on dissenters influenced other university presidents in their response to campus disruption. "He was one of the few who had the guts to do it, and I am sure this had an affect on other university presidents. But this is typical of Ted. He's a very humane man and no one would fight harder for freedom of expression and the opportunity to explore philosophically or scientifically—but Ted did believe in the sanctity of the university," Murphy says.

"And you can't have free exploration if you've got a bunch of 'know-nothings' running around trying to tyrannize the majority. A year-and-a-half after his telegram to Hesburgh—in August of 1970—Anson was taken prisoner in Cambodia by Khmer Rouge guerrillas while covering the Vietnam war as a correspondent for *Time Magazine.* In their book Connelly and Dooley relate that Diane Anson cabled Hesburgh from Singapore imploring him to help in obtaining her husband's release. Immediately Hesburgh ". . .dispatched a lengthy telegram to Rome to request that the Vatican diplomatic service intervene with Prince Sihanouk's exile government in Peking to secure the release of this alumnus. Three weeks later, Anson was set free."[12] He showed a real sense of integrity and courage. It was the measure of the man," Murphy adds.

Yale President Kingman Brewster does not entirely agree with Murphy's appraisal and says that secular university presidents cannot wield such "peremptory" power. "I don't think it had a great deal of effect on other university presidents," Brewster says, "because very few presidents would consider themselves to be in a position where they could take disciplinary action of a conclusive nature by simple administrative fiat. Most of us have to operate through faculty or sometimes faculty-student disciplinary committees. I, myself, used the cease and desist device as part of my own scenario, but that would be simply an interlocutory order or a temporary injunction whereby pending a determination by the appropriate disciplinary committee, I could suspend a person.

"This is different, however, from what Father Hesburgh did when he said conclusively that he would ask a person to cease and desist and, if he didn't, he would be out. That kind of conclusive, peremptory authority is not shared by many people in the secular university world. But I do believe it is probably true that in terms of public opinion there was an impression that Ted Hesburgh had taken a firmer position on student unrest than other presidents had." Brewster was more impressed by Hesburgh's cable to Governor Rockefeller at the 1969 Governors' Conference opposing federal intervention regarding student behavior. "As a result," Brewster wrote in the preface to Hesburgh's Terry Lectures, "President Nixon was persuaded not to extend federal police power to the campuses of the nation."

Brewster assessed Hesburgh's rank among American university presidents. "I would rank him very high," he replied. "The test of a great university president is not his public splash, but what he accomplishes for his own institution. I think the tremendous accomplishments—physically, academically, nationally, internationally—and the status of Notre Dame University as a result of Ted's ministrations is terribly impressive. In terms of contribution to his own institution, he is one of the really significant university presidents." Dr. Franklin Murphy concurs, saying "among his contemporaries during the time he has served Notre Dame, American and international higher education, he has been one of the giants."

Ray Maddalone attended Notre Dame from 1966 to 1970 when, as he describes it, "kids grew up a lot faster." Now a research chemist doing work in energy and environmental chemistry, Maddalone recalls that the general campus reaction to the cease and desist order was favorable. "I thought everyone took it quite well," he says. "My impression was that it was well received. If you read the complete text of the order and understand its rationale, what you find is an eloquent statement in defense of individual rights."

During those volatile four years, Maddalone observed Hesburgh's handling of student unrest and the increasing demand by the students for more participation in decision-making and formulating university policy. Maddalone was considerably impressed with Hesburgh's forceful leadership. "He definitely calls the shots. He determines how much the students are going to get in terms of their freedom." But what made Hesburgh's leadership remarkable, according to Maddalone, was his sense of timing with regard to his perception of student maturity. "Hesburgh was always willing to give the students more freedom so it wasn't so much a question of student pressure. It had to be the right eloquence, the right demonstration of actual student understanding of the problem. Once that was expressed—you know in retrospect it seems like we always played the rules according to his game—he was willing to yield as soon as we had shown the maturity."

In addition, the decisions made were rooted in a judicious sympathy, according to Maddalone. "I don't think any side felt its opinions had not been fully considered," Maddalone said. "I don't think anybody felt cheated. You always had the feeling that Hesburgh had listened and truly understood your position. But it was more than that —you knew that he *cared* about you."

CHAPTER 6
THE CIVIL RIGHTS COMMISSION:
THE EARLY YEARS

In his State of the Union message in 1956, President Eisenhower asked the Congress to create a civil rights commission authorized to investigate the economic pressure being used in the South to deprive blacks of their constitutional right to vote. Eisenhower's proposal came in a political climate when the American people were becoming increasingly cognizant of the racial injustice permeating the nation. This growing awareness was essentially the result of a volatile succession of events beginning in 1954 with *Brown* v. *Board of Education,* the historic Supreme Court decision outlawing segregation in public schools. The following year, the President sent federal troops into Little Rock, Arkansas, to enforce the court-ordered integration of Central High School and to provide protection for the black students. The same year Rosa Parks refused to sit at the back of a bus in Montgomery, Alabama, an act of passive resistance which was a catalyst for sit-in and freedom ride protest movements.

The first civil rights act to be adopted in 82 years was signed by President Eisenhower on September 9, 1957. Title 1 of the new Law created the United States Commission on Civil Rights which was to be an independent, bipartisan federal agency. The Commission was empowered to investigate allegations of denied voting rights that were based on race, color, religion, or national origin; to collect information on legal developments and maneuvers that denied the constitutional guarantee of equal protection under the laws; and to evaluate the federal government's laws and policies with respect to civil rights. The commission was to report its findings to the President and Congress within two years.[1]

Little Rock had made Eisenhower only too aware of the intense passions aroused by racial division. Sherman Adams, in his book *Firsthand Report,* said that Eisenhower felt that sending federal troops into Little Rock was the most "repugnant. . .constitutional duty" he had to perform during his eight-year presidency.[2] Consequently, the President sought to appoint commissioners who, as he described, would have an "ameliorating effect" on the racial animosity which had clearly been manifested at Little Rock. At a news conference on October 30, Eisenhower said he was seeking men of "thoughtful mien" who would reflect "the spectrum of American opinion" and inspire public confidence.[3]

With these prerequisites in mind, Eisenhower selected the six commission members, judiciously respecting its bipartisan character with three Democrats, two Republicans, and an Independent. The commissioners named were Hesburgh, then just 40 and already a university president for five years; John A. Hannah, president of Michigan State University, who was designated as commission chairman; John S. Battle, a former governor of Virginia; J. Ernest Wilkins, a black who was Assistant Secretary of Labor; Doyle E. Carleton, a former governor of Florida; and Robert Storey, dean of the law school, Southern Methodist University. The commissioners were sworn in at the White House on January 3, 1958.[4]

The commission's first hearings, held in Montgomery, Alabama, in December 1958, concerned the denial of voting rights. Upon learning that the commission intended to hold such hearings, the Montgomery *Advertiser* reported Circuit Judge George C. Wallace declared that any agent of the Civil Rights Commission who tried to secure voter registration records within his two county jurisdiction would be "locked up." Wallace then impounded all registration records in the counties. Nevertheless, the commissioners (who had to stay at Maxwell Air Force Base because Montgomery's hotels were segregated) began hearing testimony on December 9. They heard witness after witness confirm in their testimonies that a silent conspiracy existed in Macon County that intended to intimidate black voters from registering to vote. In his comprehensive history of the Commission, *The Civil Rights Commission: 1957-1965*, Foster Rhea Dulles describes the testimony:

> The complaintants described their experiences in almost identical terms. They invariably experienced great difficulty in finding out when the local Board of Registrars would hold one of its infrequent sessions. They had to submit their applications in a room much smaller than that available for whites, only two could be processed at a time, and they had to wait endlessly in a standing line. All Negroes were required to copy a specified article of the Constitution and then fill out a long and complicated form. The process usually took close to two hours. A single mistake in writing the section of the Constitution or filling out the application blank—a misspelling, a wrong date, anything else—could be seized upon at the whim of the registrar to reject an application.[5]

The testimonies were at times poignant and eloquent. One of the witnesses, Amelia JoAnne Adams, a 22-year-old candidate for a master's degree in organic chemistry at Tuskegee Institute, moved the commissioners with her quiet and understated answers to their questions as to why she had never received a reply to her registration application.

> COMMISSIONER WILKINS: Do you have any opinion as to the reason you haven't heard from it?

MISS ADAMS: Well, I can read; I can write, and I think I possess all my mental faculties. So, the only thing I can think of is the fact that I am a Negro.

CHAIRMAN HANNAH: I would like to ask. . .Why do you want to register to vote?

MISS ADAMS: Well, the Government of the United States is based on the fact that the governed govern, and only as long as the people are able to express their opinions through voting will the country be able to remain the great power that it is.[6]

Hesburgh reflected the growing compassion of commission members as they listened to an unremitting narrative of intimidation described by the witnesses. An example of this can be seen in a brief interchange with a Bullock County farmer describing the futility of his attempts to register:[7]

COMMISSIONER HESBURGH: Mr. Sellers, are you going to keep trying?

MR. SELLERS: Oh, yes, I'm determined to register.

COMMISSIONER HESBURGH: God bless you.

In the Commission's second statutory report issued in 1961, Hesburgh wrote a minority statement. His intentions were not to express a difference of opinion, but rather to express his conviction that the commission had become "a kind of national conscience" concerning civil rights and that the federal government could only offer a small solution to what was essentially a bigger problem of the human heart. The statement, issued appropriately in the fifth volume of the commission's report entitled *Justice*, is an eloquent appeal to the "innate fairness. . .generosity. . .and consummate good will" of the American people to maintain their fidelity to the Judeo-Christian tradition in order to solve the race problem. The statement was unique in that a federal commissioner was articulating a philosophical and even theological approach in solving the age-old problem of race.

In giving his reasons for filing the statement, Hesburgh called attention to the inadequacy of federal action to fully resolve the problem and pleaded for the concern of every citizen and his conscience:

> I am filing this personal statement because of a personal conviction that Federal action alone will never completely solve the problem of civil rights. Federal action is essential, but not adequate, to the ultimate solution. In the nature of the problem, no single citizen can disengage himself from the facts of this report or its call to action. Leadership must come from the President and the Congress, of course, but leadership must also be as widespread as the problem itself, which belongs to each one of us. May I then say just a few words about what the Commission Report, as a conscience, seems to be saying. I claim no special wisdom. This is just one man's extra step beyond the facts of the report and its recommendations.

Hesburgh then lamented the disparity between the promise of the Constitution and the inimical existence of racial injustice in the nation:

> The most depressing fact about this report is its endless tale of how our magnificent theory of the nature and destiny of man is not working here. Inherent in the depressing story is the implication that it is not working because we really do not believe in man's inner dignity and rightful aspiration to equality—unless he happens to be a white man.

Condemning efforts to deter blacks from voting as a "crude and sorry . . . reign of terror" and censuring the equally "heartless" denial of decent schooling for blacks, Hesburgh urged the American people to be faithful to their spiritual and moral heritage.

> Perhaps we could establish a stronger alliance against these outrages if we were to meditate more deeply on the true import of our Christian heritage. Could we not agree that the central test of a Christian is a simple affirmative response to the most exalted command mankind has ever received: "Thou shalt love the Lord thy God with thy whole heart, and thy whole soul, and thy whole mind, and thy neighbor as thyself." No mention here of a white neighbor. There was another similar statement, "Whatsoever you did (good or evil) to one of these, my least brethren, you did it to *Me.*" We believe these truths or we do not. And what we *do,* how we *act,* means more than what we *say.*

Hesburgh wrote of his deep inner conviction that anything less would be hypocritical and a betrayal of the very values on which the nation was founded.:

> Personally, I don't care if the United States gets the first man on the moon, if while this is happening on a crash basis, we dawdle along here on our corner of the earth, nursing our prejudices, flouting our magnificent Constitution, ignoring the central moral problem of our times, and appearing hypocrites to all the world. . .we should as a Nation take this stand for human dignity and make it work, because it is right and any other stance is as wrong, as un-American, as false to the whole Judeo-Christian tradition of the West as anything can be.

Finally, Hesburgh solicited the nation's moral indignation:

Maybe more constructive action will come sooner if we allow ourselves the unfashionable and unsophisticated taste of moral indignation: when known murderers go untried and unpunished with the studied connivances of their fellow citizens; when brutal fear is forced even upon women and children in America; when economic reprisals are used to prevent qualified American citizens from voting, but they are not exempted from paying taxes and serving in the Armed Forces; when little children are stoned by a vicious mob because they dare to go to a decent school long denied them; when people are intimidated, embarrassed, and jailed because they presume to eat in a public place with other people; when a place for homes becomes, by neighborhood action, an empty park because Americans think they will be contaminated by Americans; when Negro Americans help pay for a new hospital and then are told there is no place in it for them; when, God help us, even at death Negro Americans cannot lay at rest alongside of other Americans.

Aware that some would think he had taken "considerable license" with the commission's mandate, Hesburgh hoped the report would not remain unread—as so many others had—by the President and Congress. He also noted that he did not think the report would climb high on the best seller list since "much of what it says is unpleasant, unpopular, and to sensitive people, a real thorn in the conscience."

CHAPTER 7
THE CIVIL RIGHTS COMMISSION:
THE NIXON YEARS

John Herbers, deputy chief of the *New York Times'* Washington Bureau and the newspaper's former assistant national news editor, covered the U.S. Commission on Civil Rights for the *Times* during Hesburgh's tenure as Chairman. Herbers, a Southerner who had a deep understanding of the problems of racial injustice and had written a book on the political disintegration of the mid-60's civil rights movements, observed Hesburgh's leadership of the commission at close range during the Nixon era.

"Father Hesburgh brought his extraordinary personal presence to bear in the cause of civil rights. He had a profound understanding of the problem which made his tenure as Chairman admirable, providing civil rights leadership much more so than anyone else at the time and against the grain of public opinion, the Congress, and the Nixon Administration. In fact, what the nation witnessed was this remarkable man putting the Civil Rights Commission on the front pages through his steadfast pursuit of racial justice in which he never yielded in the face of the negative political climate and hostile public opinion," Herbers says.

Herbers recalls the political atmosphere before and after Hesburgh was appointed chairman of the commission by President Nixon in February of 1969: "He took over the Commission at a time when it was all right to do so among his peers. Even the conservative clergy was active in civil rights in the early and middle 1960's. Priests and nuns participated in freedom marches and there was no stigma attached to such political involvement."

However, Herbers says the situation changed as civil rights became associated with the anti-war movement in the national division over the Vietnam war. "It was not as respectable to be a civil rights advocate. Members of Congress would support civil rights only if their constituents would allow it. People got tired and the saying was 'Black is boring.'"

Herbers recalls that Hesburgh was not liked by the Nixon Administration because "he made waves—he did not fit in." In fact, the only two members of the Administration who were sympathetic to civil rights, according to Herbers, were Leonard Garment and Daniel Patrick Moynihan. When Hesburgh criticized the Administration's civil rights policies, or lack of them, it was always done without partisan political overtones and in such a way that if the Administration had really been interested in promoting civil rights it could have learned from his judicious criticism. "He always tried to be constructive and he made sure he touched all bases giving the Administration ample opportunity for constructive use of the commission's criticism," Herbers says. "It was a matter of conscience for him and he made it clear that he was acting completely without political motivation. For example, he never used any elaborate public relations mechanism as most politically motivated individuals do. He was concerned about the institutional wrongs and believed the government must do what is right."

Hesburgh's presence as commission chairman was, according to Civil Rights Commissioner Manuel Ruiz, " . . . similar to Abraham Lincoln when he said a house divided against itself cannot stand. Hesburgh was deeply concerned about the distinguishing opportunities between blacks and whites. He could see that unless even abrasive action was taken to straighten this out we would be entering an atavistic era.''

Court-ordered busing set off a virulent reaction in the nation in the early 1970's. The Nixon Administration, already repaying the political debts of the 1968 "Southern Strategy" and anticipating the 1972 election, proposed anti-busing legislation in the form of a constitutional amendment (House Joint Resolution 620) and a House Bill (H.R. 13915) which would have dealt a virtual death-blow to busing in any form. Hesburgh testified against both pieces of legislation in March and July and, in doing so, aroused the administration's rancor to such a degree that the decision was made to somehow force his resignation as Chairman and a member of the Commission. Hesburgh's trenchant criticism of the administration had already proved embarrassing to the president's domestic political image, especially during an election year it was quickly becoming intolerable.

For example, in his testimony on July 28 before the House Committee on Education and Labor regarding H.R. 13915 (Equal Educational Opportunities Act of 1972) Hesburgh censured what he considered the harmful intent of the legislation:

> I must say in all candor that the title of the bill before the Committee is not representative of its content as one reads its several provisions. If this measure is designed to implement the 1954 decision of the Supreme Court requiring desegregation of racially segregated schools, it fails. If it is designed to provide equal educational opportunities to the minority group children of the Nation, it fails. If it was designed to move the Nation toward one society with justice for all, it fails.
>
> If it was designed to further fractionalize the Nation along racial lines, it succeeds. If it was designed to deprive minorities of equal protection of the laws, it succeeds. If it was intended to commit Blacks, Chicanos and

Puerto Ricans to at least another generation of second, third and fourth class educational facilities, it succeeds.

Declaring that if passed the bill would establish a "racially reactionary policy," Hesburgh said the act "hoists a false banner in its title and in its content it is oppressive. This bill burns the last bridge out of the ghetto."

Herbers said that Hesburgh's testimony before the committee "exposed the Equal Educational Opportunities Act to be what it was: a fraud." With this testimony, which was so clearly damaging to the administration's domestic political image, "the overt moves to oust him began," according to Herbers. He believed that the moves were made with the President's approval, but "whether or not Nixon orchestrated them I don't know."

Hesburgh's testimony during the March and July hearings concerning an administration-sponsored Constitutional amendment forbidding busing for desegregation included a judicious recapitulation of busing's legal and social persuasion. In the July testimony he offered a *modus vivendi* which would have significantly mitigated the intense national hostility toward busing. By stating "educational achievement is what we are really seeking," he favored a legislative provision prohibiting busing any child to an inferior school. Such a provision—whether in the form of a bill or a Constitutional amendment—would certainly have gone a long way in reducing the fears of parents who felt busing meant an inferior education for their child.

Hesburgh also told the House Committee of some interesting commission findings resulting from a study of 14 northern and southern urban and rural communities using busing to achieve desegregation. The commission found that being under court order often helped, paving the way for a superintendent and board to take a step that, according to Hesburgh, might have otherwise been "politically perilous." Also, it was found that improvements in curriculum and facilities commonly accompanied busing. "Districts are careful to see that previously neglected schools are spruced up before white pupils are transferred there," Hesburgh said. In addition, given the preconditions of community support and advance preparation of staff, teachers and students, it was found that desegregation went more smoothly at the elementary level.

Hesburgh's testimony in March was given before the House Committee on the Judiciary regarding House Joint Resolution 620 which had been introduced the year before by U.S. Representative Norman F. Lent, a Nassau County Republican. The resolution proposed the following prohibition as a Constitutional amendment:

> Section 1. No public school student shall, because of his race, creed, or color, be assigned to or required to attend a particular school.
>
> Section 2. Congress shall have the power to enforce this article by appropriate legislation.

Hesburgh perceived the resolution as not only an overt attack on busing, but as a covert assault on "just about every form of remedy which brings black and white children together in a school." He told the Judiciary Committee that the amendment would prohibit school pairing (even of near-by schools) and closing of segregated schools of inferior quality in order to integrate their student bodies; eliminate transfer provisions that allowed a child of a majority race to transfer to schools where his race is in the minority; forbid redrawing of attendance lines to desegregate schools; prohibit the busing of children for desegregation; and prevent school districts from assigning pupils on the basis of race in order to redress segregation.

To Hesburgh the proposed amendment contradicted the equal protection guarantees of the 14th Amendment under the guise of "a neutral principle" which, though appearing innocent was contextually considered not merely as "anti-busing" but both "anti-school desegregation" and "anti-black." Hesburgh described its invidious intent and the accompanying black anguish when he said:

60   **Hesburgh: Priest, Educator, Public Servant**

"Where you go to school—the quality of education you receive and
the attitude which you acquire toward learning—has a determina-
tive effect upon your life. A slum school can have, as our courts have
recognized, an effect upon children which could probably never be
undone. No wonder many blacks regard this amendment as another
way of saying 'Don't touch me, you are not a human being.'"

Hesburgh criticized the "constitutional" amendment as being
constitutionally dubious. "The 14th Amendment, as modified by
this provision," Hesburgh said, "would prohibit the States from
denying equal protection of the laws to all, except to school children." Then he cited Chief Justice Warren Burger's 1971 opinion
in *Swann v. Charlotte-Mecklenburg Board of Education* in which
the Supreme Court struck down a North Carolina statute identical
to the proposed amendment. Instead, it reaffirmed race as a criteria
to remedy segregation.

> The legislation before us flatly forbids assignment of any
> student on account of race or for the purpose of creat-
> ing racial balance or ratio in the schools. The prohibition
> is absolute, and it would inescapably operate to obstruct
> the remedies granted by the District Court in the *Swann*
> case. But more important the statute exploits an appar-
> ently neutral form to control school assignment plans by
> directing that they be "color blind"; that requirement,
> against the background of segregation would render illu-
> sory the promise of *Brown v. Board of Education* 347
> U.S. 483 (1954). Just as the race of students must be con-
> sidered in determining whether a constitutional viola-
> tion has occurred, so also must race be considered in
> formulating a remedy. To forbid, at this stage, all assign-
> ments made on the basis of race would deprive school
> authorities of the one tool absolutely essential to fulfill-
> ment of their constitutional obligation to eliminate exist-
> ing dual school systems.

Burger noted that in the absence of a constitutional violation the use of race to determine the court-ordered assignments of students is not constitutionally permissible. He said that in a society where equality truly exists the best approach "might well be" assigning students to schools nearest their homes. However, Burger wrote, racial assignment made a suitable and "proper" remedial tool in eliminating the "deliberately constructed and maintained" system of enforced racial segregation. "When school authorities present a district court with a 'loaded game board,' affirmative action in the form of remedial altering of attendance zones is proper to achieve truly nondiscriminatory assignments. In short, an assignment plan is not acceptable simply because it appears to be neutral."

Hesburgh informed the subcommittee that *Swann* was a precedent-setting decision because it was the first time that specific legal remedies were considered in creating the unitary school system since the Court mandated "separate but equal" schools unconstitutional in 1954. He then told the subcommittee that it was the court's opinion that judicially ordered busing is an appropriate remedy in school desegregation cases. Hesburgh explained that the test of how much busing is permissible is based on reason, and he quoted for the subcommittee the section of Burger's opinion defining that test: "An objection to transportation of students may have validity when the time or distance of travel is so great as to either risk the health of the children or significantly impinge on the educational process."

Hesburgh then gave the subcommittee a scholarly summary of the legal progress of school desegregation since *Brown* v. *Board of Education* and brought committee members up to date on two recent Supreme Court decisions which had severely criticized the dilatory and fragmentary progress toward eradicating unconstitutional school systems. Hesburgh specifically pointed to the 1968 *Green* v. *School Board of New Kent County* decision where the court felt compelled to speak out against the slow and piece-meal approach to the school desegregation and condemned token plans as unsatisfactory responses to the requirements of *Brown*.

In the *Green* ruling, a rural Virginia county, New Kent, had operated just two schools—one black and one white. The county school board adopted a freedom of choice plan, claiming that by its adoption it had desegregated the school system thereby complying fully with the law. However, the integration was only minimal and the Court held that the mere existence of a freedom of choice plan was not an adequate response to abolishing dual school systems as required by *Brown*. The Court said that school boards have an "affirmative duty" to eliminate dual school systems in such a way that every vestige of racial discrimination is forever uprooted. The court expressed this judicial imperative in one of those memorable legal metaphors which Supreme Court Justices seem to have a considerable gift for creating when justice is truly at stake—such as Justice John Marshall Harlan's magisterial dissent in *Plessy* v. *Ferguson* when he wrote that "Our Constitution is color blind." Justice William Brennan wrote that school boards were "clearly charged with the affirmative duty to take whatever steps might be necessary to convert to a unitary system in which racial discrimination would be eliminated *root and branch* (author's italics).

Hesburgh then told the subcommittee the opponents of racial justice had delayed the *de facto* implementation of *Brown* so gravely that by October 1969 the Supreme Court felt legally and morally compelled to issue explicit directives regarding desegregation. He cited that in August of that year, the Fifth Circuit Court of Appeals had granted a request by the Department of Health, Education, and Welfare to delay by one year the implementation of desegregation plans for 30 Mississippi school districts. Because the Nixon Administration offered no other desegregation measures in lieu of the withdrawn plans, all of the Mississippi districts would be able to continue using their old freedom of choice plans. The Supreme Court, confronted by an imminent defiance of its 15-year-old judicial mandate, decided it had had enough of the Administration's political machinations. The Court therefore revised its own "all deliberate speed" standard originally enunciated in *Brown* for implementing desegregation, saying in *Alexander* v. *Holmes County Board of Education:*

...continued operation of segregated schools under a
standard of allowing "all deliberate speed" for desegregation is no longer constitutionally permissible. Under
explicit holdings of this Court, the obligation of every
school system at once and to operate now and hereafter
only unitary schools.

Hesburgh's testimony, combined with his considerable influence
in Congress and with the public, was instrumental in the defeat of
the Administration's anti-busing legislation. In addition, just before
the November election he wrote an article for the *New York Times
Magazine* entitled "Father Hesburgh's Program for Racial Justice"
in which he said busing was a "phony issue." It is interesting to note
that in the first paragraph he quoted the newspaper's editorial
endorsing Senator McGovern for President in which the *Times'* editors obliquely spoke of the "arrogance of power" pervading American political life. Former commission staff director Howard
Glickstein says that "this was the last straw" with regard to the
Nixon Administration. The orchestrations to remove him began.

John Buggs, staff director of the Civil Rights Commission when
Hesburgh resigned as chairman in November of 1972, remembers
the circumstances of Hesburgh's resignation vividly. His narrative
of the events surrounding the chairman's dismissal is a close and
revealing look at the behavior of the Nixon White House.

Buggs recalls that on the Thursday before the November 1972
election, he received a call from the White House telling him that
all presidential appointees were to report to the Assembly Room
of the Executive Office Building at 11 a.m. on the following Wednesday, the day after the general election.

"They were so sure of re-election that they ordered the en masse
assembly five days before. However, never did the White House indi-
cate in any way whatsoever that this meeting was to include the
Civil Rights Commissioners. When I arrived at the Assembly Room
Wednesday morning, all Presidential appointees except Cabinet
officers were present. Then about ten seconds after 11:00 Erlichman came in and profusely apologized for being late. He told us the

President was meeting with the Cabinet in the Cabinet Room and was telling them exactly what he, Erlichman, was going to say to us. Whereupon without any ceremony he told us that the President wanted our resignations by Friday. Then in a very cold and offhand manner he said, 'We don't want you to go out of here speculating or giving reasons why the President asked for your resignation,'" Buggs recalls.

The entire meeting only lasted about five or six minutes and as each appointee left the room he received a large manila envelope with his name on it containing instructions for resigning. The packet included a "Post-Election Activities Memorandum" telling the soon-to-resign appointee that the purpose of the resignations was "to give the President a free hand to strengthen the structure of government as he begins his second term." The memorandum, which was stamped "Administratively Confidential," noted that although the requested resignation would take place during a period of "some uncertainty," it was anticipated that "all major actions on person-nel will be completed by December 15" and, therefore, there was no need for any anxiety (the uncertainty "will be dispelled as quickly as possible"). Then as a stern parent might chastise his child, the memorandum said in severe and condescending terms:

> Between now and December 15, please plan on remain-ing on the job, finishing first-term work, collecting and depositing Presidential papers, and making plans for next term. This is not a vacation period.

A second memorandum entitled "Disposition of Personal Papers" followed and told the requested resignee that:

> No matter what your plans, the President is most con-cerned that a very valuable record of the Presidency is likely to be dispersed or destroyed. For those of you expecting to depart the Administration, he requests you to give your personal papers to the United States for

eventual deposit in the Richard Nixon Presidential Library.

Included next in the packet was a resignation preference form complete with several boxes to check indicating the resignee's own future plans with regard to the Administration—to remain "if the President wishes"; "in my present position"; "in another position"; "stay only under certain circumstances"; or to have his "resignation accepted." The final enclosure in the packet instructed appointees to secure *pro forma* letters of resignation from all Schedule C employees (those appointed by the Presidential appointees themselves).

After receiving the packet, Buggs went back to his office at the Civil Rights Commission, wrote his own resignation, gathered those of his own appointees and sent them back to the White House.

On Monday, November 13, the commissioners met in executive session with Hesburgh presiding. Buggs was present along with the executive staff. Two commissioners, Maurice Mitchell and Manuel Ruiz, Jr., were absent. The long morning meeting began early and was proceeding as usual when at approximately 10:25 a.m. the phone rang. Buggs picked up the receiver. It was the White House calling for Buggs himself. The voice on the other end was that of a woman (Buggs cannot recall her name or whether or not she was a secretary) who said she was calling at the request of Fred Malek, special assistant to the President.

Buggs knew immediately that such a call was ominous. Malek, then 35, a West Point graduate and former Green Beret, was in charge of personnel at the White House and was known, according to Buggs, as the "headhunter." In *The Time of Illusion*,[1] an historical account of the Nixon era, Jonathan Schell says that Malek could issue punitive decrees or bestow indulgences depending of course on which Cabinet aide or government official was in or out of the president's favor. (For instance, Malek could, according to Schell, dispense engraved White House invitations to state dinners to those officials who needed a morale boost and withhold such emoluments from others whom, as Malek himself phrased it, "we may want to get rid of."

The woman asked Buggs, "Why haven't we received the commissioners' resignations?" Buggs recalls that her voice was "not intimidating" but he knew exactly what she was getting at and, therefore, he tried to conceal with whom he was talking by lowering his voice and giving monosyllabic answers. "Here I was in the middle of a meeting with the commissioners, and she was asking why the White House had not received their resignations," Buggs says.

Buggs told her that he was not aware that the commissioners' resignations had ever been requested by the White House.

"Did you ask for them?" she queried.

"I was not aware that this was expected of me. In fact, my explicit instructions were to hand in my own resignation and then secure the resignations of my own appointees," Buggs replied.

"Well, you were supposed to."

"I told you I was never informed that I was to do this."

"Will you tell them now and then get the resignations?"

"I will do no such thing."

Buggs said the only thing he would do would be to give the commissioners the message. "By this time it was damned apparent to the commissioners sitting around the conference table that I was getting steamed," Buggs recalls.

"Will you tell them that we want their resignations by Wednesday?" the caller said.

"I don't think that is possible because they live in different parts of the country," Buggs replied. (The commissioners were leaving for home immediately after the meeting.)

"I looked over at Father Ted and could see he was getting suspicious of what was going on," Buggs remembers.

Buggs then told the woman, "If the White House had wanted the commissioners' resignations in the first place they should have asked for them. No request for their resignations was ever forthcoming nor was there even an indication that the resignations were desired."

After the call was over, Buggs told the commissioners that the White House was demanding their resignations *en masse*. He recalls Hesburgh's reaction to the news: "I don't think I had ever seen him get so angry. He was remarkably quiet but his face and manner revealed how he felt inside. He was deeply hurt and disturbed." Hesburgh said little, according to Buggs, except for one comment: "If they want my resignation they shall have it as soon as I return to Notre Dame."

Commission Vice-Chairman Stephen Horn, unaware of what the White House's real design was, told a reporter, "Hell, the whole government has resigned. There's nothing to it. It wasn't even Malek, it was some clerk."

The next day, Tuesday, Buggs left for commission hearings on Indian rights in Albuquerque and Phoenix. When he arrived in Albuquerque on Wednesday morning and checked into his hotel he found a message waiting for him from the White House. He was to call a White House staff assistant immediately. Buggs ignored it and went out to the hearing. At the noon recess reporters converged on Buggs because they had heard rumors that the White House was demanding the resignation of Father Hesburgh as chairman. Buggs confirmed the story telling them about the phone call and the precipitous ultimatum demanding the *en masse* resignation of the commissioners.

"When I got back to my hotel room that night the White House called again. It was the staff assistant," Buggs says. The staff assistant opened the conversation by saying, "Mr. Buggs, why didn't you call me back? I not only called you at the hotel this morning but twice at the hearing."

"I'm sorry, but I was too busy to return your call," Buggs replied.

The White House deputy then explained the reason for the call. "We have not received Hesburgh's resignation nor those of any other members of the commission. Did you give them the message?"

"I did."

"Well, in case they did not receive or understand it for some reason, will you tell them again?"

"I don't think I would like to do that. If the White House wants their resignations then it is up to the White House to call each commissioner and ask for his resignation personally. You can call my office at the Civil Rights Commission and get their phone numbers."

That ended the conversation and Buggs went to bed. He finished the hearings on Thursday and went to Phoenix on Friday for the next hearing. During the hearing itself Buggs was interrupted by another phone call from the White House. It was the staff assistant again.

"Well, I see you've been talking to the press."

"Yes, I have. They asked me questions, and I answered."

"There are no resignations yet."

"I'm sorry about that. I do know of one commissioner who has written his. I know of another resignation I don't think you are going to get and that is Manuel Ruiz."

The conversation ended abruptly after this. "It was pretty obvious that the object of this call was to intimidate me and get me to keep my mouth shut," says Buggs.

At 6:45 Saturday morning Buggs was awakened out of a deep sleep by the ringing of the phone. He picked it up groggily and heard the voice of the staff assistant again who this time was speaking in conciliatory tones.

"Did you tell the press that we had requested the resignations of all the commissioners other than just Hesburgh's?

"I told them that the White House had requested their resignations *en masse*. Those were the instructions conveyed to me through Malek's office."

"You were mistaken, weren't you?"

"I don't understand."

"Mr. Buggs, no one ever told you to ask the commissioners other than Hesburgh for their resignations."

"You've got to be kidding!"

"We have no record of any such request, Mr. Buggs."

"Listen, on Monday a woman from Malek's office called me during a commission meeting and told me to tell the commissioners that they all must resign. Then I spoke with you yesterday and on Wednesday, and both times you yourself asked for the resignations."

"You must be mistaken, Mr. Buggs, and you would do us a great favor if you would correct that to the press."

"Well, I guess the you-know-what has finally hit the fan."

"No, no, no, no—nothing like that. You just made a mistake and we understand that. If you'll just correct it."

"I will do no such thing!"

Buggs says that after his unequivocal refusal the White House deputy made no further attempt to coerce him into a lie. "There was no remonstration, no threat. I had been very emphatic that I would do no such thing. Yet I couldn't believe their audacity nor how they thought they would ever get away with it. The whole conversation was so incredible that I thought perhaps I was dreaming or hearing things," Buggs reflects.

The White House had misrepresented what had happened. The *New York Times* on Friday had reported that the White House Press Office understood that "the five other members of the commission had not been asked to resign, that they were considered in a special category and thus were not included in the President's request." Presidential Press Secretary Ron Ziegler offered a gratuitous explanation: "There are no plans to gut the commission." The following morning Buggs received the phone call from the White House demanding that he tell the press that only Hesburgh's resignation had been requested. But with Buggs' refusal, the White House was forced to concede that it had indeed requested the resignation of the five other commissioners as well.

Commissioner Manuel Ruiz, a top Los Angeles Mexican-American attorney specializing in international private law, did not resign. He was the first Mexican-American to attend the University of Southern California Law School from which he graduated in 1930. After receiving his degree he went into practice by himself because of the pervasive prejudice against those with a Mexican or Spanish surname among law firms in Los Angeles. "They didn't want anyone with the disability of being a Mexican-American because it wasn't in keeping with the prestige that was required by those law firms," Ruiz recalls.

Ruiz had received news of the resignation from Buggs over the phone. He had been preparing for the hearings on Indian rights and had been unable to attend the commission meeting in Washington. In response to the resignation request Ruiz wrote an ingenious letter in the form of a memorandum to his colleagues on the commission. The letter was addressed to Buggs and was written from his law office in Los Angeles. Aware that a written legal agreement cannot be modified verbally, Ruiz used his legal acumen as well as the stratagems for survival he had learned as a Mexican-American lawyer in writing the letter which read:

MEMORANDUM TO THE COMMISSIONERS

SUBJECT: Resignation

Dear John:

I have been contacted by the Press as to whether I will tender my resignation under the change of the Administration.

My answer will be that I was personally appointed, in writing, and that a request for my resignation should be received by me in an instrument of equal dignity.

Since the appointment required the intercession and the approval of the Senate, even as is the procedure for appointment to the United States Supreme Court, it is my opinion that a different rule applies, and that a simple general request is not self-executing insofar as the Commissioners are concerned.

Yours truly,

Manuel Ruiz, Jr.

"I was not going to resign unless I got a personal request from the President himself. Of course, that was never forthcoming," Ruiz explains. "The President had a problem on his hands. Obviously, he didn't want Hesburgh there but he couldn't request one resignation because that would be too apparent. So the White House thought if all the commissioners resigned, then the President could select the resignations he desired and say to the press whatever reason he might have in mind at the time he accepted Father Hesburgh's resignation. But it didn't quite work out that way."

The White House's offensive against Hesburgh surfaced from its surreptitious veiling and was carried on in full public view from the office of the President's press secretary. On Thursday, November 16, the day Hesburgh was drafting his formal letter of resignation at Notre Dame, Assistant White House Press Secretary Gerald Warren gave a press briefing and said the White House staff had requested the resignation of Father Hesburgh because he had said during the presidential campaign that he would resign if President Nixon were re-elected. That night Hesburgh wired the White House and issued a statement of defending himself and refuting Warren's statement.

> Despite recent irresponsible news articles to the contrary, I did not—repeat not—say that I would resign if President Nixon were re-elected. When asked to comment about this story at the time, I simply denied it. What I did say was that if I were asked to resign by the re-elected President, as is his privilege, I would. He did ask, and I did resign. After 15 years of service on the Civil Rights Commission, I would appreciate having the record honestly stated.

Former staff director Howard Glickstein recalls what Hesburgh did say when asked during the campaign why he did not resign. According to Glickstein, Hesburgh replied, ''Well, if I do resign they'll probably appoint some rabbit in my place.'' In a *New York Times* article on the resignation, John Herbers wrote that Hesburgh had been quoted as saying he could ''not survive if the President was re-elected—either by his wishes or my own.'' Glickstein said that such commentary did little to ''endear him to the Administration.'' In fact, it was probably the acerbic nature of the remarks which induced the White House to distort what he said. (The Nixon White House was then at the height of its power—having just won one of the largest pluralities in American political history—and it did not receive such astringent observations with equanimity.)

Hesburgh attempted conciliatory approaches to the President, telling Leonard Garment that if he could get in to see him he could perhaps explain the full dimensions of the problem to him. Garment was not able to get him an appointment, however. Former staff director Howard Glickstein recalls that even when the impasse between Hesburgh and the President had reached its most severe level, the chairman attempted a reconciliation. "Sometime in late '72 just before he was fired Hesburgh was invited to a reception for the President. He wasn't sure whether he should go, but finally decided that it would be in bad taste in his position as Chairman not to go. He went to it hoping that perhaps he would have some opportunity to speak with the President about their disagreements over civil rights. Hesburgh went through the receiving line and when he reached Nixon the only thing the President said was 'How's Parseghian?'" (Ara Parseghian, then the Notre Dame football coach).

Hesburgh became the only commissioner whose resignation was accepted, thus becoming the first presidential appointee to resign as the President entered his second term under the announced reorganization of the government.

Hesburgh's letter of resignation to the President was a terse one-sentence instrument of compliance:

November 16, 1972

Honorable Richard M. Nixon
The White House
Washington, D.C.

Dear President Nixon:

In compliance with your request, transmitted by Mr. Frederick Malek of the White House staff, I hereby submit my resignation as Chairman and member of the U.S. Commission on Civil Rights.

Best regards.

Cordially yours,

(Rev.) Theodore M. Hesburgh, C.S.C.
President

cc: Commissioners
   Mr. Buggs

Thirty-five days later the President sent Hesburgh a "Dear-Ted" letter accepting his resignation and expressing his "deep gratitude" for his 15-year service on the Commission. The letter reads:

December 20, 1972

Dear Ted:

It is with deep gratitude for your contributions to the well-being of our nation that I accept your resignation as Chairman and Member of the U.S. Commission on Civil Rights, effective November 17, 1972.

As a leader of the Commission for nearly fifteen years, you have worked courageously and tirelessly to advance the civil rights of every American.

In spite of the systemtic difficulties, to which you have often referred, great progress has been made over these years. But neither of us can be satisfied while so much remains to be done.

In 1976 we will celebrate our nation's 200th Birthday. In that remarkable document which stated to the world our purpose and resolve, Jefferson wrote of the "unalienable Rights" endowed to each of us. Through your devoted work, you have helped to protect and perfect these rights, and for this I join with every American in expressing my deep appreciation.

With kindest personal regards.

Sincerely,

Richard Nixon

Commission Vice Chairman Dr. Stephen Horn recalls his reaction when the President's letter was read before the commission members. "The letter that President Nixon wrote Hesburgh after he was sacked as Chairman is the most glowing letter that could ever be written to any public official," Horn says "You wonder if the President knew that the White House staff was removing him, because the dichotomy was so unbelievable that I broke out in laughter when it was read during a commission meeting. Ordinarily, you don't write a letter like that to someone you have just summarily dismissed. You wonder if the President knew what was going on. On the other hand, the President might have known everything and personally ordered it himself. Who knows?"

The President's peremptory discharge of Hesburgh enabled him to weaken the Commission's moral and political influence with Congress and the public for some time. There was no one of equal stature on the Commission who could galvanize public opinion and directly influence members of Congress in the way Hesburgh did.

Hesburgh's abrupt dismissal, according to Manuel Ruiz, left the Commission in a state of disarray. "In the absence of Hesburgh," says Ruiz, "the Commission was leaderless for a great period of time. Naturally, there was confusion. Our Vice Chairman, Stephen Horn, was an excellent commissioner, but he didn't have the national recognition that Hesburgh had. This opened the way for those within the Congress who were against Civil Rights to gather their forces in an attempt to phase the Commission out of existence.

"When Congress established the Commission in 1957 it was created in such a way that it would self-destruct in a couple of years. One of those built-in structural creations was the stipulation that the commissioners would receive no salary. They figured that a lot of retired old fuddy-duddies would be appointed. But instead they got some real activists, much to their surprise. They got people who weren't worried about whether their salaries would be cut off because they had their own independent sources of income. The Congress also divided the Commission into Republicans and Democrats hoping they would argue among themselves and be unable to function as a body.

"When the Commission was originally organized the thought was that it would function as a kind of token gesture or perfunctory obeisance to civil rights. Senators and congressmen would invite their oppressed constituents to testify before it and pretend to be interested in what they had to say. Then the politicians could wash their hands of the problem and say to the voters, 'Well, I've referred this over to the U.S. Commission on Civil Rights,' thinking that that would be the end to it. But it wasn't. They never expected the Commission to last beyond two years. They never anticipated that the Commission would be able to actually sit down as a body to study and work on the problem. Fortunately, the Congress made one mistake—a good one for the Commission—and that was to give it the power to subpoena. With this power there was nothing that would keep the Commission from going out and getting answers and putting those who discriminated on the hot seat."

With Hesburgh's dismissal as Chairman, the position remained vacant for 16 months, until the appointment of Arthur Flemming, former Secretary of Health, Education, and Welfare under Eisenhower, was confirmed by the senate in March of 1974.

Hesburgh, along with the help of McGeorge Bundy at the Ford Foundation, created a center for Civil Rights at Notre Dame. The center, which is located at the Notre Dame Law School and has been called a "civil rights commission in exile," has indexed Hesburgh's papers collected from his 15 years on the commission. Howard Glickstein, who was the center's first director, said that the center would make a significant contribution to the writing of American civil rights history. In addition, Hesburgh hoped that its presence at the law school would make the university a focal point for civil rights in general. "The good law schools in the country are all thought as perhaps prepared to specialize in one thing, like torts or international law. It is my hope that our contribution will be civil rights or at least how it emerged through the work of the commission," he explains.

Any solution to the racial injustice permeating American life must, according to Hesburgh, be rooted in a remedial approach that includes housing, education, and employment. "I call it that sad trilogy which is at the heart of progress in civil rights," he says. "Now if you don't receive a good education you'll never find a good job. If you don't have a decent-paying job than you will never have enough money to buy a decent house in a decent neighborhood. Your children will then be in an unsatisfactory house in a depressed neighborhood where they will receive an inadequate education. The circle of discrimination and poverty goes around and around continuing with incessance generation after generation. No one within the circle can break through its circumference into the economic, social, and educational mainstream."

One of the first things Hesburgh believes should be done to interrupt this destructive cycle is to efface the disintegrating inner core of the cities by a radical dispersal of the population to new communities beyond urban environs. The maldistribution of land used for living space can clearly be seen in the fact that today three-quarters of the nation's population lives in concentrated urban areas constituting only three percent of habitable land. This dispersal could be accomplished, according to Hesburgh, through planned communities with open housing conventions and connected to areas of employment by rapid transit. Housing experiments similar to this have already been successfully attempted in communities such as Reston, Virginia, and Columbia, Maryland.

Until this dispersal can be achieved, Hesburgh contends, busing should be used as a "limited tool." "What we have to do is temporarily use whatever expedient methods that are available to get all of our children in good schools," he says. "Busing may be the only answer for some children, especially black children. The great proportion of blacks live in the inner cities where the schools are poor. How can anyone deny a child a decent education just because he is unfortunate enough to live in an area where the schools are impoverished?

"Some people ask, 'Why don't you create good schools in the ghetto?' and I answer by saying that we've had two hundred years of ghettos, certainly enough time to create good schools there. I don't have very much hope that this will be accomplished next week or next month. Sure, there are good schools in the ghetto, but they are by and large parochial schools. I don't know of any great public schools in the ghetto.

"People are screaming about busing today. Well, I say to them that the Supreme Court put it very well when it said a child should not be bused if it means he or she will receive a worse education. If it means a better education, there isn't a parent, black or white, who would mind the bus ride for his child. In fact, more than one-half of the nation's children ride to school on a bus."

Hesburgh refused to comment on Dr. James Coleman's sudden reversal with regard to busing. It was Coleman's famous report on educational opportunity in 1966 which prepared the way for massive busing plans in school districts throughout the nation. "Coleman is going to have to explain his reversal. I thought there was truth to what he originally said but there is apparently some problem with his evidence. However, since it is *his* position that is reversed, I would rather not comment and let him explain it himself."

CHAPTER 8
PRESIDENTIAL
CLEMENCY BOARD:
ELOQUENT CONSCIENCE

In the long history of Anglo-American jurisprudence, the pardoning power and its investiture in the office of the head of state is most eloquently stated in *The Federalist Papers* No. 74 written by Alexander Hamilton:

> But the principal argument for reposing the power of pardoning, in this case in the chief magistrate, is this: in seasons of insurrection or rebellion there are often critical moments, when a well-timed offer of pardon to the insurgents or rebels may restore the tranquility of the commonwealth; and which, if suffered to pass unimproved, it may never be possible afterwards to recall.

Apparently the framers of the American Constitution were moved by Hamilton's argument, because Article II, Section 2 of the Constitution reads, in part, that the President "shall have the Power to grant Reprieves and Pardons for Offences against the United States, except in cases of impeachment."

American presidents have exercised this discretionary power with both prudence and compassion. In 1778, before the Constitution had been ratified, Thomas Jefferson, then a member of the Virginia House of Delegates, introduced a "Bill Granting Free Pardon to Certain Offenders" which called for a "full and free pardon" for Americans who had either joined the British forces or abetted the British cause. In the bill Jefferson noted that the American Congress had passed a resolution on April 23 recommending "to the good and faithful citizens of these states to receive such returning penitents with compassion and mercy, and to forgive and bury in oblivion their past failings and transgressions." It was the clement view of the Congress, Jefferson said, "that the people of these states are ever more ready to reclaim than to abandon, to mitigate than to increase the horrors of war, to pardon than to punish offenders." Jefferson himself was the first American president to grant a pardon to military deserters.

The pardoning power was first exercised by a president when George Washington granted a "full, free and entire pardon" in 1795 to all the insurrectionists involved in the Whiskey Rebellion and later to the rebellion's ringleaders, who had been convicted of treason. In explaining his use of the power in the Pennsylvania insurrection, Washington said:

> For though I shall always think it a sacred duty to exercise with firmness and energy the Constitutional powers with which I am vested, yet my personal feeling is to mingle in the operations of the government every degree of moderation and tenderness which the national justice, dignity, and safety may permit.

In 1800 John Adams pardoned another group of Pennsylvania rebels involved in the Fries Rebellion of 1779, including the principal agitator, John Fries, who led the uprising against the federal tax collection and had been sentenced. Andrew Jackson extended executive clemency to war deserters in 1830, forcing Congress to repeal the death penalty for peacetime desertion.

Perhaps the most poignant expression of presidential clemency is found in Abraham Lincoln's handwritten pardons issued during the Civil War. These terse orders pardoning Union Army deserters are suffused with an appeasing mercy:

> This boy having served faithfully since, is pardoned for the old desertion.

> If David Levy shall enlist and serve faithfully for one year, or until otherwise honorably discharged, I will pardon him for the past.

> If Henry Stork of 5th. Pa. Calvary has been convicted of desertion, and is not yet executed, please stay till further order and send record.

> Let the unexecuted portion of the sentence be remitted and the soldier be returned to duty with his regiment to serve his full enlistment, including period of absence.

Lincoln was frequently confronted at the White House by a deserter under sentence of death who placed himself at the President's mercy. Moved by the man's plight, Lincoln would telegraph a full pardon to the soldier's commanding general with the provision that the reprieved soldier faithfully serve out his term of enlistment. Not all received pardons, however, and 141 Union soldiers were executed for desertion.

Fifteen years after the end of World War I, President Franklin Roosevelt issued a "Christmas Amnesty Proclamation" pardoning and restoring citizenship rights to those who had completed prison terms for violating draft or espionage laws during the war. Four amnesty proclamations were promulgated by President Truman which granted executive clemency to World War II Selective Service violators and peacetime deserters, as well as restored the civil rights of ex-convicts who had served faithfully in the armed services.

Thirty-eight days after assuming the presidency from Richard M. Nixon, President Gerald Ford offered conditional clemency to the

draft evaders and military deserters of the Vietnam War saying that
he was fulfilling a personal promise "to throw the weight of my
Presidency into the scales of justice on the side of leniency and
mercy." The President explained the urgency of his decision:

> I did this for the simple reason that the long and divi-
> sive war in Vietnam has been over for American fight-
> ing men, more than a year, and I was determined then
> as now to do everything in my power to bind up the
> nation's wounds. . .I do not want to delay another day
> in resolving the dilemmas of the past, so that we may all
> get going on the pressing problems of the present. There-
> fore, I am today signing the necessary Presidential
> proclamation and executive orders that will put the plan
> into effect.

Ford said that the primary purpose of his amnesty program was
"the reconciliation of all our people and the restoration of the essential unity of Americans," a unity without which only "angry discord" and "excessive passion" would prevail because of the
profound national division over the war. The President then stated
his rationale behind the program, the intent being to return the
deserters and evaders to their communities and families, integrat-
ing them back into American society through a period of alternate
service: "Desertion in time of war is a major, serious offense; failure
to respond to the country's call for duty is also a serious offense.
Reconciliation among our people does not require that these acts
be condoned. Yet, reconciliation calls for an act of mercy to bind
the nation's wounds and to heal the scars of divisiveness."

To achieve this reconciliation, the President issued an executive
order establishing a nine-member President Clemency Board to
review the records of draft evaders and military deserters on a case-
by-case basis. He appointed as chairman 48-year-old former U. S.
Senator Charles E. Goodell, a Republican who had been politically

ostracized by the Nixon Administration because of his strong opposition to the Vietnam War.

The others named to the board were Hesburgh, who had called for an unconditional amnesty; General Lewis W. Walt, 61, the retired assistant commandant of the U.S. Marine Corps who had been the Marine Corps commander in Vietnam; Vernon E. Jordan, 39, black civil rights leader and executive director of the National Urban League; James Maye, a paralyzed former Marine Corps flight officer wounded in Vietnam who was executive director of the Paralyzed Veterans of America; Robert H. Finch, 51, Nixon's former Secretary of Health, Education, and Welfare who later served as a Presidential Counselor; Dr. Ralph Adams, president of Troy State University in Troy, Alabama, and a brigadier general in the Alabama Air National Guard; James P. Dougovita, 28, a Vietnam veteran who was a teaching aide for minority students at Michigan Tech University and a captain in the Michigan National Guard; and Aida Casansas O'Connor, 52, a lawyer who was assistant counsel to the New York State Division of Housing and Community Renewal in New York City.

The President's proclamation was directed toward the 113,337 civilians and servicemen who had evaded the draft or left the military between the adoption of the Gulf of Tonkin resolution on August 4, 1964, to the withdrawal of the last American combatant on March 28, 1973. Of that number, 100,115 were fugitives or discharged AWOL offenders and 13,222 were unconvicted or convicted draft offenders.

All applicants were required to earn clemency by performing up to 24 months of alternative service where appropriate. Unconvicted draft evaders were under the authority of the Justice Department and were to report to the U.S. Attorney. Upon completion of alternate service, charges against them were dropped or the indictment was dismissed.

Unconvicted military absentees were to report to their respective military service and take an oath of allegiance to the United States. After agreeing to alternative service, prosecution would be foregone and an undesirable discharge issued. The absentee would then receive a Clemency Discharge upon completion of alternative service.

Convicted draft evaders and convicted military absentees were to apply for clemency to the newly created Clemency Board. The Clemency Board, depending on the review of each case, would recommend clemency to the President. The clemency would either be unconditional or conditional, using a period of alternate service. The President would then grant clemency and in the case of military deserters, substitute a clemency discharge for a punitive or undesirable discharge.

The composition of the Clemency Board was such that a tenuous balance existed between liberal and conservative approaches to clemency. In selecting the original nine members (later expanded to 18) the President selected a group representative of the schism which had divided the American population during the war in Vietnam. Some members such as Vernon Jordan, had come to oppose the war and as a result of his experience on the board, would support an unconditional amnesty. Others had reservations about amnesty.

Chairman Charles Goodell, regarded as fairly liberal due to his early opposition to the war, waived the role of advocate in order to better balance and mediate any irreconcilable disputes that might arise. It was a wise decision on his part in light of the angry impasse that developed between the board's two most notable members, Hesburgh and General Lewis Walt, whose equally resolute approaches to clemency were paradoxically opposing and similar.

It was in these fiercely fought debates that Hesburgh emerged as the board's conscience, moving the members by his eloquent pleas and commanding presence.

New York Times reporter Diane Henry, who covered the Clemency Board during its early days, recalls that it was the general consensus among the press that if Hesburgh was indeed the conscience of the board, it was due to his tempering the views of General Walt whose reputation with regard to clemency was "Neanderlithic." Walt, a four-star general, had been the Marine Corps commander in Vietnam and later assistant commandant of the Marines. He had spent over 30 years in the service and firmly believed that his role on the board should reflect the tradition of military discipline. His decisions on the board were a major deterrent to future draft evaders and military deserters. Associate General Counsel James Poole remembers that Walt would "explode" during board sessions and at times would want to give "more than the appropriate form of punishment." James Maye confirms this description in recalling one disputed case where Walt recommended no clemency whatsoever, giving Maye the impression that the General believed "flogging" to be the more appropriate response to the man's desertion.

General Walt was not, however, without sympathy and compassion for the plight of the common soldier who had deserted. Foremost among all of the commanders in Vietnam, he was known as the "soldiers' soldier," a commander who had been in the field and understood combat pressure. He knew what it meant when a lieutenant gave an order in the field which would well mean either the man's life or his death.

Walt was revered with uncommon affection by the troops he commanded. An example of this affection was witnessed by Special Counsel Richard Tropp as he was going into the Executive Office Building for a Clemency Board meeting. "As I entered through the guarded entrance, one of the secret service security guards asked me when General Walt would be coming. I told him the General would be coming in a few minutes and he explained that he had served under Walt in Vietnam and wanted to give him a gift in appreciation for his leadership."

It was in their empathy for the common soldier that, despite all their differences, Hesburgh and Walt found a common ground. "Both Hesburgh and Walt had a unique feeling for the problems and plight of the individual involved. They approached clemency from a different set of assumptions and objectives. Yet they were able to find a common ground because they both had a gut sense of the real problems of the deserters," Tropp says.

"Walt had been tempered by his experience on the battlefield and by his everyday contact with the common soldier. Hesburgh had been on the All Volunteer Army Commission and understood the plight of these men. He had an intuitive feel for their problems," Tropp explains.

Their mutual concern for the deserter's or evader's individual fate, however, did not deter either man from expressing and arguing with passionate conviction his views on clemency. The result was a virtual standoff between the two which often erupted into angry exchanges of great intensity. Their diverging moral approaches to clemency could not be approximated, let alone negotiated. This was unfortunate for the board as a whole since a cohesive policy on clemency was dependent on the views of its two most pre-eminent and forceful members. The disparity between their opposing views became so serious that, had it remained so, the board probably would not have been able to function. Goodell realized the gravity of the impasse and called in James Maye to act as mediator.

Maye was a former flight officer in Vietnam who had been seriously wounded during the Tet Offensive and paralyzed from the waist down. Having seen the war from both sides—as participant and victim—Maye was considered to be the board's "swing vote." Goodell had been impressed by his quiet intelligence and thought that Maye's dual perspective on the war could help bring a *modus vivendi* between Hesburgh and Walt.

Maye remembers the call from Goodell. "I was approached when the problems between the two were insurmountable," he remembers. "Goodell told me that the situation was untenable and asked me to take it. I was at a loss. There I sat a total unknown between a four-star general and the renowned Father Hesburgh. I was familiar with the immense reputation of both men and had admired them from a distance. Now I was in their middle. It was a vastly over-whelming experience. General Walt felt he was being forced into a corner and that his beliefs were being compromised. Hesburgh felt the same way. I didn't have any well-defined approach—just logic and common sense. General Walt threatened to resign. He told me he couldn't deliberate under the circumstances. He thought the board was weighted on the liberal side. He said Hesburgh gave the liberal side too much leverage, and he thought it had been left to him alone to give the conservative viewpoint a sufficient strength."

The severity of the tension between Hesburgh and Walt was a manifestation of the nation's political and emotional climate at the time. The last American combatant had left Vietnam only 18 months earlier. The memory of the war was very painful. An American President had just resigned leaving his unelected successor to govern a spent and divided nation. The emotional and moral beliefs of its citizenry had become entangled in a series of recriminating fabric resulting from the strain of Vietnam and Watergate.

Maye remembers vividly the emotional climate in the three-man panel in which clemency became a deeply felt moral issue for both. "There was tremendous aggravation and stress between them," he says. "The arguments were fierce. Tempers flared. Emotions erupted as the frustration between them grew. Both men were capable of great moral indignation and were willing to put up with any condition imaginable to support their convictions. The problems confronting them were intricate. The moral issues they were addressing were not simple at all. Hesburgh's emphasis was on the individual, giving him the benefit of the doubt. Walt was conditioned by the system and the individual was seen in that perspective with little variance from that point of view.

"The interesting thing is each man saw a little of himself in the other," Maye adds. "At a cocktail party you would probably find them together with a couple of drinks in hand talking about hunting and fishing. They are both men of strong will and immense self-discipline. Both are capable of violent indignation and compassion at the same time.

"For example, I have always thought that if Hesburgh were walking in a back alley and was jumped by a mugger, he would be torn between two courses of action. Either he would give him all of his money because the attacker needed it, or he would beat the hell out of him in order to straighten him out morally. And Walt—despite his stern newspaper reputation as the prototypical Marine commander—has a tremendous capacity for compassion. While he was in Vietnam he built at least 10 hospitals for children with money from his own pocket and funds he raised among the troops."

Maye says that each man recognized his own self-discipline in the other, although that very discipline caused them to react differently to the same situation. "It was a classic example in psychology of different reactions to the same stimuli. With all of his self-discipline Hesburgh could say to himself, 'I can understand the weaknesses of others.' While Walt would say, 'If I can discipline myself, why can't others?'"

Maye remembers that he finally went to Hesburgh and told him that Walt's opinions had a certain validity. Hesburgh listened to Maye and agreed that the General's views did possess a certain validity at times. "Hesburgh's view was not a myopic one. He had a malleable mind and during a discussion he would change his mind saying 'maybe you were right,'" Maye says.

Special Counsel Richard Tropp, a Yale Law School graduate and legislative assistant to Goodell when he was a Senator, remembers that it was Hesburgh's personal presence which was the board's pivotal focus. "He was a commanding presence," Tropp says. "Others on the board would turn and listen to him if they were undecided. Hesburgh was extremely eloquent and this tempered the views and feelings of the other board members. He saw and felt the individual's problem and emotionally identified with it. He was able to express the plight of the person and make it intelligible to the other members of the board, persuading them by the force of his eloquence."

Maye remembers one disputed case in which Hesburgh and Walt would not yield to each other. The case involved a soldier who had apparently deserted under fire in Vietnam. "He had a multitude of problems," Maye recalls. "Serious family difficulties had contributed to his emotional instability. The question was whether he had deserted in a combat zone or a rear area.

"The General took a hard line and recommended no clemency whatsoever. Hesburgh, however, noted some mitigating circumstances and recommended clemency. Neither man would yield, and there was no way to resolve the impasse between them. So the case was remanded to the full board where Hesburgh made an eloquent plea and won, overriding the General by his clear and concise explanation of the soldier's plight.

Hesburgh told the board that the record showed the young man had served well in previous combat, but that under the combined duress of combat pressure and family stress, he had finally broken. "There were no hard facts whether it was a combat zone or a rear area," Maye recalls. Hesburgh argued that the pressure of combat, combined with his family problems, was such that he could have been either in a rear area or a combat zone and he would have deserted.

The first six months of the board's existence was spent in formulating policy. "In the early days of the board," Tropp recalls, "we had tremendous battles struggling to fit the criteria together on the length and kind of alternative service and in deciding what would be aggravating or mitigating circumstances. Hesburgh was especially effective in bringing to bear a sense of what a rule would mean. He would pose arguments with respect to a rule to see what effect it would have on an applicant." The deliberations were so volatile and involved such intense personality testing among board members, according to former Associate General Counsel James Poole, that Goodell called the board into closed executive sessions and even excluded top level staff from attending.

It was particularly difficult for the panel because the differing approaches to clemency among its members had to be translated into a workable program that would not only prove acceptable to a divided nation but also to its clement purpose. Both Hesburgh and Goodell suffered severe personal criticism at the hands of some political liberals for participating in President Ford's clemency program. "They were vilified and subjected to personal attacks in print, by letter and phone, from certain elements of their own liberal constituency who felt they had capitulated by joining a program which did not go far enough," Tropp says.

"The American Civil Liberties Union and some liberal church organizations were particularly hard on them. However, both men deserve inestimable credit because despite any reservations they themselves had about the President's program (Hesburgh himself was on record at that time for an unconditional amnesty), they believed that there were individuals who needed and could be helped by it. They simply put their heads down and took the flak," he explains.

Of the 21,729 persons applying for clemency under the President's program, 15,468 were Clemency Board applicants. Under the Clemency Board 4,620 military deserters and 1,432 draft evaders received outright pardons; 7,252 deserters and 299 evaders received clemency contingent on some form of alternative service; and 885 deserters and 26 evaders received no clemency at all.

On January 21, a day after assuming the Presidency, Jimmy Carter issued a proclamation granting a "full, complete and unconditional pardon" to draft evaders of the Vietnam era. Left unresolved was the fate of the nearly 100,000 men who entered but then deserted the armed forces during the Vietnam war. The President said he would begin study of possible review processes for military deserters.

Of the Clemency Board, Hesburgh says, "It was one of the toughest programs I ever took part in because of the enormous requirement of personal time and effort. Every one of the more than 15,000 cases we received had to be reviewed individually, and most of them had a file two or three inches thick. It's a terribly costly way to do business from the point of view of those making the judgments. We finally broke up into teams of three and even then it took an enormous amount of time, because we were trying to get through 100 cases a day and then go home and prepare the next 100 for the following day. It was just the most time-consuming way of performing our duties. There must be an easier way.

"I was always in favor of an unconditional amnesty simply because the war was ill-begotten in the first place. It may well be that those who resisted were more courageous from a moral point of view than some of those who went," Hesburgh continued. "And those who waged it most fiercely like President Nixon got off scot-free as did many of the people who were on his team. Even Mr. Agnew got off scot-free. If those at the heart of it escaped with impunity, why should those who got caught in its tentacles down the line be punished?"

In January 1976 the Ford Foundation gave Notre Dame's Center for Civil Rights a $225,000-grant to study the problems of Vietnam war veterans, military deserters and draft evaders. One of the objectives of the study is to examine the system of American military justice with regard to the fact that an estimated 500,000 servicemen who went absent without leave during the war and the estimated 175,000 soldiers received undesirable discharges.

CHAPTER 9
UNIVERSAL SOCIAL AND
ECONOMIC JUSTICE:
A VISIONARY SCHEMA

The social dimension of the Gospel is a salient concern of Hesburgh's theological vision of the world. He believes that the Gospel must be efficacious in the temporal order as well as the eternal. For Hesburgh, God's justice is not extraterrestrial: "I have always believed that you have to work for justice on earth and not just in eternity. We recreate conditions for the Kingdom of God here on earth in preparation for the Kingdom in Heaven. When you are working for justice, for human freedom, for human rights, and for human development, you are indeed working for the Kingdom of God."

Hesburgh would like to see a shift of emphasis in Catholic theology from orthodoxy, which focuses on doctrinal concerns, to orthopraxis, which reflects on the Christian vocation to serve others in the *oikoumenè* or inhabited world.

Catholic theology has been gradually turning to this emphasis, most notably with Pope John Paul II's encyclical *Laborem Exercens.*

John Paul II views labor as the continuation of the work of creation: "The word of God's revelation is profoundly marked by the
fundamental truth that man, created in the image of God, shares
by his work in the activity of the creator. . ." (*Laborem Exercens*
Para. 25) The summons to cocreation is found in the Book of Gene-
sis, where human beings are called to "subdue the earth."[1] With
this universal summons to share in the work of the Creator, according to John Paul II, there is a correlative call to subdue economic
and social injustice among nations: "The disproportionate distri-
bution of wealth and poverty and the existence of some countries
and continents that are developed and of others that are not, call
for a leveling out and for a search for ways to ensure just development for all."[2]

Dutch theologian Edward Schillebeeck declared that "the hermeneutics of the Kingdom of God consists in making the world a
better place." Peruvian theologian, Gustavo Gutierrez believes
Christian witness must be a "theology of liberation" which seeks
social, economic, and political justice reflecting the Heavenly
Kingdom.

In Hesburgh's Terry Lectures at Yale given in 1974, he concluded
the first lecture, which he termed an "*apologia pro vita mea*" or
statement in explanation of his life, with the following passage from
Gutierrez' *Theology of Liberation*.[3]

All the dynamism of the cosmos, and of human history,
the movement towards the creation of a more just and
fraternal world, the overcoming of social inequities
among men, the efforts, so urgently needed on our con-
tinent, to liberate man from all that depersonalizes
him—the physical and moral misery, ignorance and hunger, as well as the awareness of human dignity, all these
originate, are transformed, and reach their perfection
in the saving work of Christ. In Him and through Him,
salvation is present at the heart of man's history.

Hesburgh ended the lecture with a reverent petition: "May we all be a part of this evolving history, this creative and salvific act."[4]

This regard for the world and its evolving destiny is reflected in Hesburgh's concern for the developing nations—the Third and Fourth World countries. He believes that only by helping them improve their crises of food shortage, overpopulation, housing, and education, can they achieve true social and economic justice.

For example, as a traveler in his nomadic journeys and as a member of the Rockefeller Foundation Board and Chairman of the Overseas Development Corporation, he has observed hunger and famine at close range—from the Sahel (the sub-Saharan region of West Africa) to the Atacama Desert (the great arid region in Northern Chile and Southern Peru). Seeing emaciated children and adults with no tangible hope for survival has filled Hesburgh with a profound anguish as evidenced in his description of a summer visit to three Sahelian countries—Senegal, Mauritania, and Mali: "I looked into the faces of hungry men, women, and children living on the edge of the desert. After four years of practically no rainfall, their animals had all died, depriving them of milk and meat and their whole nomadic way of life. Here one learns that behind the dismal statistics there is a human condition that demands a solution . . . There are few sights more heart rending than human beings without food or drink. One understands, in seeing them, the premium the good Lord placed on feeding the hungry and giving drink to the thirsty."[5]

Hesburgh's feelings run so strongly about solving the problem of hunger, that he is undaunted by any government official or bureaucratic red tape. For instance, Civil Rights Commission Vice Chairman Dr. Stephen Horn recalls the time when Hesburgh was conducting civil rights hearings in St. Louis and was informed of the Nigerian conquest of Biafra.

"We had gone back to our respective rooms, and both of us had tuned in the television newscast for that evening. On the screen was the junior-grade director of Nigeria who had just defeated the

Biafrans. The Biafrans were starving—their plight was inhuman,''
Horn says.

''We had planned to have dinner that evening, as we often did—
two college presidents who would talk shop at the end of the day.
As we were getting into a taxi to go to a restaurant both of us
expressed our mutual outrage. Then Father Ted said to me, 'Why
don't we call Elliot Richardson (who was then Undersecretary of
State) and say the United States should do something about this?'
I said that was a good idea, and we both looked for a phone booth,''
Horn recalls. ''Then Father Ted said, 'If I could do anything about
it, I would gather a group of leading Americans and get right into
the cockpit of an American airplane and land it in Biafra tomor-
row with all the food needed to save those people from starving.'
I said I agreed with him, and so we got into a phone booth and
reached Richardson through the White House switchboard. I don't
know if he thought we had something to drink, but we hadn't—
we were both just wound up with moral outrage on what was
happening in this African country where people of the same nation-
ality were starving others because they were on the losing side in
the civil war.

''We made our suggestions to the undersecretary, and I regret to
say to no avail. Later it was revealed that the State Department staff
had sold the department's leadership a bill of goods on that situation, which wasn't quite correct,'' Horn concludes.

Hesburgh is pragmatic enough to know that such moral spon-
taneity succeeds only infrequently given the bureaucratic inertia
of government. Consequently, he offers a three-part approach to
the problem of hunger.

Because every year there will be a food crisis somewhere in the
world, due to natural disasters such as floods, droughts, or earth-
quakes, Hesburgh proposes storing 10 million dollars worth of emergency food storage for disaster relief. The United States, which
supplies 80 percent of world food exports, should put up at least
half of the emergency storage.

Second, Hesburgh proposes a concerted buildup of world food stocks and reserves for protection against a bad weather disaster in the American midwest or Canada. The U.S. has only a 30-day reserve supply of food stock. According to Hesburgh, a worldwide natural disaster that included the United States, Canada and Australia would permit only a 30-day grace period before serious hunger problems developed worldwide.

Hesburgh's third approach is long-range and in his opinion the most important. "We simply have to teach people how to grow food where they live, right where the hunger is," he declares.

While visiting the Sahel on a food relief mission, he surveyed the various means being used to feed people. "The methods they were using were so anachronistic and primitive it was like feeding an elephant with an eyedropper," he observed. Hesburgh looked for long-range solutions and discovered a plan that was sensible, yet was not being implemented. The plan included building two dams on the Senegal River, one near the mouth to prevent salinization, and one up river. "The upriver dam would have the capacity to provide irrigation for up to a million acres of the region's arid land, feeding all six of the Sahelian nations and doing it quite expeditiously," Hesburgh says.

Hesburgh believes it is only common sense for our government to support such proposals. In the first place, he says, teaching people to grow food for themselves eliminates the complication and expense involved in transporting grain from, say, Iowa or Kansas to Bangladesh or Senegal. In addition, he believes the arable land in the United States is now approaching the limits of fertilization. "Putting one more pound of fertilizer in Iowa is not going to make that much difference. However, if we do it in Bangladesh or India we can get ten pounds more food since they are so underfertilized," he explains. Hesburgh cites as an example the comparative grain production between the United States and India. The area of land under cultivation between the two is the same, but due to the United States' advanced fertilization methods, the ratio of grain actually cultivated is twice as much for the U.S.

The problem of grain production and fertilization techniques has been a longtime concern of Hesburgh's. His familiarity with the great agricultural programs of the Rockefeller, Ford, and Kellogg Foundations has made him keenly aware of the historic potential of agricultural development.

He has visited the International Rice Research Institute (which was established by the Rockefeller and Ford Foundations) near Manila several times and notes in *The Humane Imperative* that he has never ceased "to wonder at what has been accomplished in so short a time, and at such a relatively low price."[6]

The Institute has classified and stored every one of the more than 10,000 species of rice, gathered 250 of the best species, genetically crossing them to get the best hybrid. It has produced new fertilizers which are so inexpensive even the poorest farmer in a developing country can afford them.

One of the Institute's first hybrids, IRRI-8, when planted on the same land, yielded a rice crop worth $1.3 billion more than the previous year's production. A year later over $3 billion more in crop yields was produced. Hesburgh says that since then more than a dozen additional improved varieties of rice and wheat have been produced and that in Asia between 1966 and 1970 the arable land cultivated by such hybrids has grown from 41 thousand to almost 44 million acres.

Aware of the revolutionary results from such agricultural research, Hesburgh worked vigorously with Harrison Brown, international vice president of the National Academy of Sciences, and George Harrar, then president of the Rockefeller Foundation, to restore a tropical agricultural research project which had been a joint undertaking of the Academy and the government. In studying the research findings, Hesburgh noted that although the scientific conclusions were superb, the project was politically impractical. Refunded by the Rockefeller Foundation, Hesburgh and his colleagues worked to make it more politically feasible, and succeeded in reinstituting the government's support. They also garnered the support of Canada, Great Britain, and Germany.

Hesburgh distributed the project's new tropical grain hybrids during the Kennedy Administration when he helped Jerome Wiesner (President Kennedy's science adviser) and several other Presidential advisers in alleviating West Pakistan's critical food shortage. They devised a plan which gave Pakistan 42,000 tons of the new short-stemmed durum wheat seed developed at the Rockefeller Foundation's tropical agriculture research station in Mexico (Centro International de Mejoramiento de Maiz y Trigo). Four years after the seeds had been sent, Pakistan was confronted with a more pleasant task—where to store the surplus wheat the new seed had produced.

Several other tropical research stations have been established under the leadership of Dr. Harrar, including the Centro International de Agricoltura Tropical at Palmyra, in the Cauca Valley of Colombia; International Institute for Tropical Agriculture at Ibadan in Nigeria; International Crop Research Institute for Semi-Arid Tropicas in Hyberabad, India; and a potato center in Peru.

As an educator, Hesburgh was especially concerned about producing foods rich in protein in view of the severe damage done to a child's brain development and his nervous system as a result of nutritional deficiency. "By age one and a half, a child has all the brain cells he will ever have. Some poor Indian children get only about 500 calories a day during the first five years of life. Wherever this is happening, we are diminishing human mental capacity irreparably," Hesburgh writes in the *Humane Imperative*.

Since the world is largely protein starved and meat is not available in many areas, Hesburgh believes unorthodox solutions such as the development of vegetable protein substitutes and new ways of producing animal protein must be found. One such approach is the planting of tilapia, a milk fish, in the irrigation canals of rice fields, which can be harvested with the rice. As a result, the protein yield could be increased by millions of tons in countries where it is lowest.

However, in order to implement the widespread use of the higher protein-yielding plants, animals, and fish, the research information and new agricultural techniques must be disseminated according to the indigenous needs of a developing country. One model for disseminating these techniques is the Rockefeller Foundation's International Agricultural Development Service. The service will evaluate a country's situation, advise them on what kind of crops, seed, fertilizer to use given the particular country's climate and soil.

The self-help approach is an integral part of Hesburgh's understanding of the problems of developing nations. In explaining his approach he is fond of quoting Ghandi on agricultural development: "Give me a fish and I eat today. Teach me how to fish and I eat every day." In pure pragmatic terms, Hesburgh believes it is just plain common sense to take such an approach: "We just can't consider that the world will always be waiting on American handouts. That's not the way to run it."

Helping the developing nations solve their agricultural problems will not be accomplished on the technical level alone. The complex maze of vested economic, social, and political interests must be reformed and restructured in order to liberate all of a country's resources in the production of food. Hesburgh believes problems such as land usage, credit, marketing, and housing should also be reformed in order to free the farmer's productive ability. "You have to get land reform in most of these countries, a better life for the farmer. He has to get a bigger share of what he grows. Rather than paying what he earns in taxes or to loan sharks, the farmer must receive better credit and marketing access," Hesburgh says.

According to Hesburgh, the generation which enters the 21st Century will face—with its attendant population growth—the imminent decrease of arable land for food crops and grazing herds. In order to truly resolve the food shortage the earth's great desert regions—which compose one-third of the terrestrial land mass—must be reclaimed for agricultural use.

As permanent Vatican representative to the International Atomic Energy Agency in Vienna, Hesburgh has had the opportunity to observe many proposals involving the nuclear reclamation of agricultural resources. One proposal which particularly impressed Hesburgh was that of Alvin Weinberg, director of the U.S. Oak Ridge National Laboratory. At the eleventh session of the IAEA in Vienna in September of 1967, Weinberg proposed employment of fast-breeder nuclear reactors to power a series of agro-industrial complexes constructed on the periphery of the earth's great arid regions. The fast-breeder reactors would provide electrical energy and water desalination for irrigation and fertilization of the arid lands. Fortunately, many of the great desert regions are in close proximity to salt water—the Sahara, the northern Sinai, the Atacama in Chile and Peru, Shark's Bay area in western Australia, and the Guajarat Peninsula in India.

In his paper before the IAEA Weinberg wrote: "One can now visualize a new kind of desert agriculture, conducted in units so highly rationalized as to be designated 'food factories' rather than farms. In these food factories, plants would be watered and fertilized at precisely the right time, and in precisely the right amounts." Weinberg explained that the food factory would employ other new "intensive chemical" processes such as electrolytic hydrogen to produce ammonia for fertilizers, the reduction of iron ore by hydrogen, electrolytic refining of bauxite to produce aluminum, or the production of caustic or chlorine to make polyvinyl chloride plastics. Industry as well as agriculture could be developed, thus strengthening the country's economy.

Hesburgh studied Weinberg's plan intensely and developed his own hybrid of the proposal in order to help resolve the Arab-Israeli conflict in the Mideast. He proposed that fast-breeder nuclear reactor installations be built in both Israel and Egypt with these complexes feeding into a common electrical and water grid irrigating the Sinai and opening it up to agriculture and industry. The Palestinians, he suggested, could be given first choice of the newly fertilized land and, with proper credit arrangements, each Palestinian family would be given twice as much land as they had lost along with special provisions for exiled children born since the first Arab-

Israeli war. The Arabs and Israelis themselves would have a literal common ground in which to perhaps achieve the mutual interest diplomats require for the negotiation of a peace settlement.

"I originally made the proposal in an Op-Ed piece in the *New York Times* after returning from Israel in 1967. I had talked about it to Aba Eban and other Israeli officials. After the article was published I suddenly received mail from all over the country saying it was a great idea and that I should do something about it," Hesburgh recalls. "I spoke about it with Lewis Strauss, who was the former head of the Atomic Energy Commission. He had gotten the same idea simultaneously while I was in Israel. He had discussed the subject with President Eisenhower, who was then in retirement at Gettysburg. Strauss had a resolution supporting such a plan put through the Senate but nothing happened.

"I talked to a gentleman who was working on it in the Mid-eastern Crises Committee, but he said it was not economically viable. I replied, 'Well, is a war economically viable?' and told him that giving the Arabs and Israelis a common interest in the Sinai was perhaps the only way we could avoid war."

Moreover, as Hesburgh writes in *The Humane Imperative:* "The Israelis have all the technology and have done some marvelous work in the desert such as the new drip-method underground irrigation system which they pioneered. This system uses only 60 percent as much water as open-ditch irrigation and avoids the plague of schistosomiasis which has afflicted the great irrigation projects at the Aswan Dam in Egypt and the Volta in Ghana."

Hesburgh believes that his plan could be financed worldwide through international bonds and its development managed and overseen under the aegis of the International Atomic Energy Agency. He also envisions giving the Agency control over plutonium residue precluding its use in developing atomic weaponry. From the standpoint of mere survival Hesburgh believes that proposals such as Weinberg's and his own will eventually be accepted. "The world would have been further along and much closer to peace today had these projects been initiated years ago. However, I think it will come some day because a third of the world's surface is semi-arid and not given to agriculture, and we have already used up most of the earth's arable land," he says.

It is Hesburgh's opinion that in 1976 Henry Kissinger finally began to appreciate the problems of the developing nations. Previously, Hesburgh believes, Kissinger gave undue emphasis to *realpolitik* and the power struggles between Russia, China, and the United States. "Before 1976 Kissinger had not even stepped foot in Latin America or Africa. Last year he finally did after going to the special session of the United Nations in the fall of 1975 and giving a fine address with over 40 suggestions on how we might edge toward a more just international economic order. It really turned the climate of confrontation between the U.S. and the Third World around at the time and gave U.S. foreign policy a more positive direction," he explains.

The direction of U.S. foreign policy in relation to assisting developing nations is one of Hesburgh's chief concerns and he will not hesitate in criticizing any administration or government official he believes is responsible for its misdirection. For example, the United Nations General Assembly had voted by a decided majority to condemn Zionism as a form of racism. As a result of this bizarre vote, the Ford Administration announced that foreign aid grants would be contingent on the potential recipient's votes for or against the United States and the United Nations. After Daniel P. Moynihan left his post as Ambassador to the United Nations in order to return to Harvard and run for the U.S. Senate, Hesburgh wrote an article for the Op-Ed page of the *New York Times* criticizing the Ford Administration's coercive use of foreign aid, a policy which, Hesburgh noted, had "apparently originated with Ambassador Moynihan." "The Administration's decision," Hesburgh wrote, ". . .to use all United States aid, including development assistance, to punish or reward poor countries that vote against us or support us in the United Nations seems to have been triggered by the United Nations vote linking Zionism with racism, a silly and stupid resolution that deserves little more than to be condemned and summarily ignored."

Calling the Administration policy a major setback for U.S. foreign relations, Hesburgh declared it immoral because it subordinated the health and survival of millions of suffering human beings to transient political issues.

The policy could only be selectively applied, since certain countries such as Brazil, Egypt, Pakistan and Nigeria—all whom voted for the Zionism resolution—possessed raw materials on which the U.S. depended. Only the "Guayanas and Tanzanias of the world" would suffer under this policy because they did not have sufficient political leverage.

Hesburgh, who was then chairman of the Overseas Development Council, directly challenged the Ford Administration by saying he would withdraw his personal support of its development aid programs if this policy continued. "If the Administration wants a political slush fund, our current programs of security assistance provide such a tool. For my part, I will have no further interest in supporting bilateral aid if it is to be used for political manipulation rather than for the improvement of the human condition in the poorest countries on earth," he wrote.

To Hesburgh the policy suffered not only from immorality but from inexpediency as well. He explained that the developing nations would now oppose any U.S. position in international forum to prove its independence from "U.S. neo-imperialism."

Hesburgh enlarged further on why such a punitive policy would be injurious to a developing nation. "The reason why it's terribly immoral and inimical to the purposes of foreign aid is because development requires a reliable flow of aid over a period of years to support long-term changes," he said.

Hesburgh explained that once aid is cut off, technicians are brought home, research work is terminated, construction projects are stopped, and university programs are severed. All momentum is lost.

He gave one example where a U.S. program was designed to bring education programs via synchronous communications satellites to 5,000 rural villages in India. A satellite was moved from a course where it passed over the Caribbean to a path above Africa's Lake Victoria where it could beam television programs into those Indian villages.

The Indian government was producing the educational programs on a wide variety of subjects including health, child care, nutrition and agricultural production. Hesburgh said that just as the project was going into effect, the U.S. government became angered over remarks made by Mrs. Ghandi concerning the CIA. As a result, the United States pulled out of the program and moved the satellite back to its original position over the Caribbean.

What makes this punitive attitude so pernicious, according to Hesburgh, is the harmful reversal of values involved in venting our anger. "We were not doing this for Indira Ghandi but for poor people, the hundreds of millions of them who need our help and support. Granted that sometimes these poor people live under regimes that are not very pleasing to us, the point still remains, are we helping the regime or the people themselves?"

The American withdrawal from the program disturbed Hesburgh for another reason. Had the program been carried through, the Indian satellite would have been the successful prototype for a global educational television network which Hesburgh proposed in *The Humane Imperative*. Hesburgh took note of the ability of American space technology to launch three synchronous satellites located above the Equator at three positions equidistant from each other with the capability of transmitting television programs to any place on earth.

Three educational data banks, Hesburgh told the Yale audience, could be positioned on earth below each satellite. The data payload would contain courses in several languages taught by the best teachers from every field of knowledge. Using a personal reminiscence, Hesburgh explained the possible benefits of his proposal: "I cannot remember a clearer lesson in my life than that about the transuranium elements from Glenn Seaborg, for he discovered and predicted most of them".

Hesburgh's viewpoints on social and economic justice gather controversy even in his own backyard at Notre Dame. South African divestment had been a controversial issue at Notre Dame. Controversial because Hesburgh believes that divestment means loss of moral leverage with U.S. companies in South Africa.

"If we do sell stock, we'll lose all influence with these companies. If American firms pull out, they'll be bought up at 50 cents on the dollar by Japanese and German firms that couldn't care less. Business will go on, albeit under leadership that doesn't care," he told *Notre Dame Magazine* in the winter 1985/86 issue.

However, there are a good number of Notre Dame students and faculty who support full divestment. They contend that only economic pressure brought by divestment will force the government to end apartheid. The division on campus reached a critical point in October 1985 when Hesburgh spoke at an anti-apartheid rally on the steps of the Administration Building.

More than 500 students—some chanting "divest now"—heard Hesburgh say that divestment would negate Notre Dame's moral influence on South African institutions. Calling apartheid "an evil system," Hesburgh said the easiest answer was "divest now." The harder question he said was "After divestment, what now?"

The university's official policy is one of "selective divestment." As set forth by the Board of Trustees Ad Hoc Committee on South African Investments, the policy prohibits investments in companies selling goods and services to the South African police, army or government; companies making loans to the South African government or its agencies; banks or institutions selling or trading South African Krugerrands.

A key provision of the policy forbids investment in companies that have not signed the "Sullivan Principles," a set of guidelines created by the Rev. Leon Sullivan of Philadelphia. The guidelines mandate that American companies in South Africa desegregate.

The Ad Hoc Investment Committee also has required companies in which the university holds stock to sign the Sullivan Principles.

Eleven companies refused, and the university withdrew the stock from its portfolio.

The views of the Ad Hoc Investment Committee were not unanimous. Three members of the committee dissented in a letter to Thomas Carney, then Chairman of the Board of Trustees. Two student members of the committee, Patrick Baccarum and John Ditting, and Peter Walshe, professor of government and director of African Studies, declared the policy "seriously inadequate on the central issue of divestment."

Walshe, a native South African, told *Notre Dame Magazine* (Winter 1985/86): "An investment policy that refers to some vague possibility of divesting at some unknown future date will not do. It is unworthy of the leading Catholic university, and it is likely to tarnish Notre Dame's image as an institution committed to the pursuit of truth and justice."

Walshe maintains that the university set a deadline whereby the South African government must commit itself to end apartheid. If not met, the university should call upon companies in which it holds stock to withdraw from South Africa and if they refuse, it should divest from those companies.

Hesburgh and other divestment opponents such as Oliver Williams C.S.C., assistant professor of management at Notre Dame, believe a critical moral dimension will be lost if the university divests. Williams maintained, "There is a moral dimension to economic decisions, and our investment in companies in South africa are moral only if they are clearly advancing the welfare of blacks in the country. In my judgment, most U.S. companies in South Africa use their corporate power to advance the welfare of blacks, and therefore the investments are moral and ought to stay."

Latin America is an area of the world for which Hesburgh has great affection. He has visited the Southern Hemisphere often and not merely to chastise military dictators such as Chile's Auguste Pinochet. He is well acquainted with two of the most distinguished politicians in Latin America, former Venezuelan president, Rafael Caldera, and former Chilean president, Eduardo Frei. "Father Hesburgh has many friends in Latin America and has always maintained a special inter-university relationship with Andres Bello Catholic University in Caracas," Caldera says. Dom Helder Camara, archbishop of Recife, Brazil, and one of the hemisphere's foremost defenders of civil liberties against the repression of military regimes, came to Notre Dame at Hesburgh's invitation in June 1976 to receive an honorary doctor of laws degree.

Hesburgh believes that the United States should be especially concerned with Latin America, because it is its "hemispheric neighbor." "If we had taken the $150 billion we dropped into Indochina and used so harmfully, channeling it instead into Latin America, it would be an entirely different world today."

Hesburgh believes that President Kennedy's Alliance for Progress was a step in a positive direction. Though the project was aborted, Hesburgh applauds its effort. "The fact is that even the effort to do something was so welcome to Latin Americans," he says. "In the poorest villages in Southern Chile or Argentina, for example, you'll see pictures of Jack Kennedy that have been cut out of newspapers and pasted on the wall of mud huts. So somehow the word got out that someone was concerned about them. Granted that not much came of it, at least the effort was better than nothing."

In May 1985, El Salvador President Jose Napoleon Duarte was the Notre Dame's commencement speaker and received an honorary degree. A member of the class of 1948, and the first Notre Dame graduate to become head of state, Duarte called on the graduates to "apply Christian theory in promoting international social justice."

Awarding Duarte the honorary degree was controversial, and Hesburgh received criticism for the decision. Students and faculty opposing U.S. intervention in Central America felt that Duarte was not significantly different from El Salvador's right wing elements which they themselves abhorred.

Duarte was first elected President of El Salvador in 1972 winning by an overwhelming majority. However, almost immediately a group of military officers seized power. The police savagely beat Duarte about the face, fracturing his skull and cheekbones. Desperate and fearful for his brother's life, Rolando Duarte called Father Hesburgh who had taught Jose theology as a student. Rolando pleaded with Hesburgh to use his contacts to have Jose removed to a neutral country.

According to correspondent Georgie Anne Geyer in *Notre Dame Magazine* (Summer 1985), Hesburgh called a former high ranking intelligence officer in California. The former officer told Hesburgh to give him an hour, saying someone would call him but not to ask who.

Geyer reports that within a half hour, someone did call. The caller said Duarte would be sent across the border to Guatemala in a weakened condition but that he would survive. The caller explained, according to Geyer: "We got in touch with the presidents of Venezuela and Panama. And they called the general in charge of Salvador and told him that if Duarte did not live, when it was *their* time to be overthrown and to look for 'sanctuary,' they would see to it that they got sanctuary in no Latin American country."

In the preface to Duarte's autobiography, Hesburgh acknowledges that in writing the preface he would expose himself to severe criticism.[7] Noting that neither Duarte nor his programs are perfect, Hesburgh contends that Duarte is "an honest man, vowed to justice and a better life for his people." Hesburgh states that Duarte inherited a culture of violence and in attempting to eliminate the violence has become a target of both the Left and the Right. Duarte seeks the political center between the "Right of the old oligarchy-military coalition and the Left, whose guerrillas want to wrest power violently by civil war. . .", Hesburgh writes.

Duarte claims today to have gained control of the military forces and gives them credit for protecting the March 1985 elections. Hesburgh was an observer at the March 1982 and March 1985 elections.

In the preface, he attests that changes in the military attitude have taken place saying that they did help protect the integrity of the elections.

During an inspection of election procedures in 1985, Hesburgh came across a funeral cortege and witnessed a poignant sight—a mother mourning for her son killed in the civil war. "There was no priest with the burial party, so I blessed the mutilated body of a young soldier who was defending the right of the people to vote and did what I could to comfort the mother. This was the pain and tragedy people were longing to be free of," Hesburgh writes.[8]

Hesburgh believes it is indeed possible to work with military dictatorships because none are the same. He is willing to help those impoverished majorities of the world whose needs cannot wait for the kind of government Americans would like them to have. "I remember talking to a Latin American dictator once and telling him what a terrible regime he was running," Hesburgh says. "He was a fairly open fellow and I could speak with him in that manner. I believe he had studied at West Point and so he knew our country fairly well. He said to me, 'I have a mass of illiterate peasants under me. If you'll trade all those peasants with me in exchange for high school graduates, I'll run a democratic government. I would find it very difficult running a democracy when the populace can't even read a ballot. To enable them to cast a vote you have to give them a symbol in the form, for example, of a red chicken or cow.'

"Sure, I think we can deal with them," Hesburgh continued. "The reason is because they are not all the same. The military government is very repressive in Chile and the regime in Brazil has been given to torture. We still must wait and see in Argentina but that situation was so chaotic it was almost inevitable that the military would step in there. Someone has to. However, the Peruvian regime has been a fairly benign military government in many ways. They have cooperated with us on some programs. And although they are a terrible bureaucratic regime to deal with, we have been able to work with them. There are others as well. "Military governments are certainly not what one would like for long range human development, but sometimes the affairs in those countries are so chaotic that the military seems like the only recourse."

As quoted by former Venezuelan President Rafael Caldera, "Father Hesburgh is a man who thinks in terms of the future." To think in those terms is characteristic of the great theological virtue of hope discussed by Aquinas in his *Summa Theologica:* "Eternal happiness does not enter in the heart of man perfectly, that is so that it be possible for a wayfarer to know its nature and quality; yet, under the common notion, that of the perfect good, it is possible for it to be apprehended by a man, and it is in this way that the movement of hope toward it arises. Hence the Apostle (St.Paul) says pointedly. . .that hope *enters in, even within the veil,* because that which we hope for is as yet veiled, so to speak."

It is with this *hope* that Hesburgh has called for a Declaration of Interdependence in which the onerous social and political demarcations caused by national sovereignty are themselves circumscribed by universal citizenship. "What I suggest," he writes in *The Humane Imperative,* "is that everyone in the world be allowed to hold dual citizenship—to be a citizen of the nation in which he or she happens to be born and, in addition, to be able to qualify for world citizenship." Qualification for world citizenship would be based on the belief in the unity of humankind and the equal dignity of every human being. Hesburgh, of course, is pragmatic and realistic enough to know that he is leaving himself open to the scoffers and cynics. Yet this is of little concern to him because this promise is rooted in *hope, even within the veil.* As he concluded the *Terry Lectures:*

> Having traveled across the face of our beautiful planet, having traversed all its oceans and its continents, having shared deep human hopes with my brothers and sisters of every nationality, religion, color, and race, having broken bread and found loving friendship and brotherhood everywhere on earth, I am prepared this day to

declare myself a citizen of the world, and to invite everyone everywhere to embrace this vision of our inter-
dependent world, our common humanity, our noblest
hopes and our common quest for justice in our times
and, ultimately, for peace on earth, now, and in the next
millennium.

CHAPTER 10
SELECT COMMISSION
ON IMMIGRATION

In October 1978, the Congress created the Select Commission on Immigration and Refugee Policy. Rising numbers of illegal aliens from America's southern borders and increasing refugee pressure from Southeast Asia made immigration and refugee policy reform imperative for the United Sates.

The Commission's charter included the study and evaluation of existing immigration and refugee laws as well as proposing administrative and legislative reforms to the President and the Congress.

The composition of the 16-member board was selected by both the President and the Congress. Four public members (including the Chairman) were appointed by the President; four Senators (by the president of the Senate); four Representatives (by the Speaker of the House); and four Cabinet officers (Secretary of State, Attorney General, Secretary of Labor, Secretary of Health and Human Services) were stipulated Commission members by law.

President Carter originally appointed former Governor Reubin Askew of Florida to head the Commission. However, Askew held the position briefly, resigning in May of 1979 when the President asked him to become U.S. Trade Representative.

Not wanting to leave his post until the right successor had been chosen, Askew met with the Commission's Executive Director Larry Fuchs to prepare a list. According to Fuchs, the top name on the list was Hesburgh's. Askew told President Carter he would not accept the appointment of Trade Representative unless Hesburgh was named Commission Chairman. President Carter agreed and directed Vice President Mondale to offer the position to Hesburgh. Hesburgh accepted and assumed the chairmanship in October 1979.

Fuchs says Hesburgh played a pivotal role in forging a new consensus to change American immigration and refugee policy. (Hesburgh was already familiar with U.S. refugee policy having worked with AFL-CIO President Lane Kirkland in a national volunteer effort to aid refugees in Southeast Asia.)

According to Fuchs, the new consensus would become the "key pillars" of the historic 1986 Immigration Reform Act, which offered:

- Employer sanctions to enforce the legislation.
- Acceptance of the principle of a secure system of employee eligibility (i.e. identity cards).
- Amnesty for illegal aliens who had entered the country before a certain legislatively determined period.
- Guest-worker program with labor standards and strong legal protection for the rights of employees.

Fuchs says that the fruit of Hesburgh's leadership of the Commission was a comprehensive and pragmatic analysis of the immigration reform issues confronting the Congress. "Hesburgh was the ideal chairman," says Fuchs. "First, he had tremendous political judgment and standing. Next, he delegated responsibility giving the commission staff the latitude it needed. He supported the staff, listened well, asked key questions, giving attention to critical details. Moreover, he was influential in formulating the issues before the

Commission. He didn't use kid gloves when he felt strongly on certain issues."

"I don't think there is any question that Father Hesburgh was the most influential member of our Commission. He was firm as Chairman in trying to steer the Commission toward its major recommendations. He did not always win on the various votes, but he won on the big ones," Fuchs concludes.

In his Letter of Transmittal submitting the Commission's second semiannual report to the Congress on September 1, 1980, Hesburgh called for a responsible immigration policy which would control undocumented/illegal immigration yet permit legal immigration for a "portion" of the world's oppressed peoples.[1]

Hesburgh stressed that as a nation, the United States could never return to the almost unlimited immigration of earlier times. He noted current migration pressures from Cambodia, Afghanistan, Ethiopia, Poland and the Caribbean. He explained that the United States could not hide from those pressures, yet stated that "we cannot be the single refuge for all of the people in the world who flee persecution or seek opportunity."[2]

He acknowledged that U.S. immigration policy was out of control with undocumented aliens coming to the United States in large numbers by land and sea. Although many of these aliens were most likely ambitious and hard-working, Hesburgh declared that their permissive entry brought the rule of law into disrepute: " . . . by permitting our laws to be flouted, we bring immigration policy as a whole into disrespect, and more importantly in the long run, we undermine respect for law, the foundation of a free society."[3]

He praised legal immigrants for their vital contributions to the economic and cultural health of the nation through their hard work, respect for law, and renewed commitment to traditional American values of "freedom, equality and family." Finally, he said that while the United States will still remain a nation of immigrants, the laws had to be enforced consistently and fairly—even when that meant not admitting some aliens and deporting others.[4]

The Select Commission on Immigration and Refugee Policy was only the second Congressional commission dedicated to immigration reform in the nation's history. The first was the Dillingham Commission established in 1907. The Dillingham Commission set a restrictive course for U.S. immigration. For example, it recommended the continuation of the exclusion of the Chinese (which lasted until 1943) as well as restrictions on Japanese, Korean and all other Asian immigrants.[5]

According to Fuchs, the Dillingham Commission was ethnically biased to the exclusion of Eastern and Southern Europeans as well as Asians. In contrast, the Hesburgh Commission viewed ethnic diversity as healthy for the United States. Fuchs states that "the choice of Father Hesburgh to replace Askew when he resigned to become the President's trade negotiator . . .was both an expression and a signal of the extent to which racism had been and would continue to be repudiated in the formulation of immigration policies. Hesburgh, known primarily for his important work as Chairman of the Civil Rights Commission, insisted from the beginning that we must design 'a policy as free of racial or ethnic bias as we can make it.'"[6]

According to Fuchs, the principal issue facing the "Hesburgh Commission" was the extensive presence of illegal aliens in the United States. Fuchs writes that it was impossible to know just how many were in the country. Demographers from the U.S. Census Bureau estimated that by the end of 1978 there were between 3.5 and 6 million undocumented aliens in the United States.[7]

In his introduction to the Commission's Final Report, Hesburgh described the Commission's philosophy regarding illegal aliens: "We recommend closing the back door to undocumented/illegal migration, opening the front door a little more to accommodate legal migration in the interests of this country, defining our immigration goals clearly and providing a structure to implement them effectively, and setting forth procedures which will lead to fair and efficient adjudication and administration of U.S. immigration laws.''

The Commission's recommendations for undocumented/illegal aliens included:

- Deportation and removal of undocumented illegal aliens to discourage early return.

- Legalization of illegal/undocumented aliens now in the United States to be determined by related measurements of residence, date of entry and length of continuous residence.[8]

The most controversial issue facing the Commission, writes Fuchs, was the employer sanctions law. Hesburgh believed that the major flaw in previous employer sanctions proposals was the absence of a secure and universal system of employee eligibility. Without such a system the full burden of legal sanctions is placed on the employer. Hesburgh favored an upgraded social security card—one that was counterfeit resistant and could only be obtained through a rigorous screening process.

Nevertheless, the Commission could not agree on the actual means to establish employee eligibility. According to Fuchs, some Commission members wanted the Hesburgh approach, others desired a new identifier system, and still others wanted a call-in system.

Fuchs notes that ''without a clear Commission endorsement for a particular mechanism—only guidelines that it be reliable, universal nondiscriminatory and cost-effective—Congressional sponsors of immigration reform legislation were unable to make a choice.''

The Congressional sponsors asked the Executive Branch to create a secure system. No reliable and secure system has yet been advanced to the satisfaction of the Congress.[9]

While determined to reduce illegal immigration, the Commission was not opposed to immigration itself. In reaching this position, the Commission was confronted by Fidel Castro's "push-out" from Mariel Harbor in the Spring of 1980. The "push-out" dramatically increased legal immigration from 526,000 in 1979 to 808,000 in 1980. This increase was due to the admission of 135,000 Cubans and Hatians and 232,000 refugees.[10] Hesburgh stated in the Final Report that the "push-out" made most Americans aware that U.S. immigration policy was out of control.

In this context, the Commission asked the fundamental question: Was immigration in the national interest? The Commission gave a strong but qualified yes. As Hesburgh explained: "A strong yes because we believe there are many benefits which immigrants bring to U.S. society; a qualified yes because we believe there are limits on the ability of this country to absorb large numbers of immigrants effectively."[11]

The Commission voted to increase numerically restricted immigration to 350,000 a year, adding 100,000 a year for five years for persons with active applications who were backlogged under the existing system.

Also, the Commission recommended that the per-country ceiling of 20,000 be waived throughout the world for the immediate relatives of permanent resident aliens.[12] Hesburgh stated that reunification of the immediate relatives should be a clear priority: "There is something wrong with a law that keeps out—for as long as eight years—the small child of a mother or father who has settled in the United States while a nonrelative or less close relative from another country can come in immediately."[13]

Therefore, the Commission recommended creating two categories. One was for immigrants whose entry into the United States would reunify families. The second placed spouses and minor children of lawful permanent resident aliens under a separate, numerically limited category without country ceilings. Hesburgh said this would help assure the reunification of families of permanent resident aliens on a first-come, first-serve basis.[14]

In keeping with its philosophy that immigration was good for the nation, the Commission also recommended the creation of a special category for nonfamily immigrants—the independent category. Hesburgh stated that the independent category "reaffirms the importance to the United States of traditional 'new seed' immigrants who come to work, save, invest, and plan for their children and grandchildren."[15]

The temporary worker issue was another difficult problem to address. Approximately 30,000 nonimmigrants entered the United States every year for short periods, primarily in agriculture. They were unprotected by any comprehensive labor standards. The Commission recommended therefore requiring employers to pay FICA and unemployment insurance for temporary workers.

Finally, the Commission endorsed the provisions of the Refugee Act of 1980 including an increase in annual normal admissions from 17,400 to 50,000. It also recommended that U.S. allocation of refugee numbers should not be provided by statute but should be provided in the course of the allocation process itself. This would allow consideration of political prisoners, victims of torture, and persons under threat of death.

The work of the Select Commission was guided by three fundamental principles: the rule of law, the open society, and an international cooperation. All three were necessary to formulate an equitable policy. The law must prevail, U.S. society must be open to new immigrants without bias or prejudice, and international cooperation must be vital because the United States could no longer accept all immigrants desiring to enter. As Hesburgh explained in the Commission's Final Report: "As important as immigration has been and remains to our country, it is no longer possible to say, as George Washington did, that we welcome all the oppressed of the world, or as did the poet Emma Lazarus, that we should take all the huddled masses of the world."[16]

CHAPTER 11
HESBURGH AND THE POST-CONCILIAR CATHOLIC CHURCH

Andrew Greeley, a knowledgeable observer of American Catholicism today, believes that Hesburgh is one of those truly great and charismatic figures with which the American Catholic Church has been favored in its brief history. "Ted Hesburgh is the most influential priest in America. He speaks for American Catholics to the outside world in a way no bishop does. In fact, he has more personal credibility than all of them put together. It is a shame he is not a cardinal," Greeley says.

Greeley says that Hesburgh is in the same intellectual and pastoral tradition as two other farsighted Catholic priests of the American Church: John Lancaster Spalding and John Ryan. Spalding was the brilliant, intellectual Bishop of Peoria in the late 19th century, a gifted writer and poet, whose independent philosophical and theological vision was far ahead of its time. Monsignor Ryan was the great labor priest of the early 20th century, whose advanced social thought provided the theoretical framework for the New Deal and whose treatise on the minimum wage laid the groundwork for its passage into law.

Greeley speculates that Hesburgh would make a superior choice as a cardinal-archbishop. "It is terrible that he has no institutional base to shape and influence Church policy," Greeley observes.

Hesburgh expresses no disappointment that he has not been made a Cardinal. He says, "It is not one of those matters which concerns me very much. I have always enjoyed being a priest and that is enough for me. No honor is greater. The real price of freedom is to be free of ambition for secular or ecclesiastical preferment. The day one starts thinking and acting with an eye to impressing the right people so as to get advanced, that day one's life becomes artificial, false, and worst of all, unfree."

Hesburgh does think about the future of the post-Catholic Church in the context of the high aspirations for the Church during and at the end of Vatican II (which in the opinion of many observers of Catholicism have never been fulfilled). Hesburgh gives an optimistic appraisal of the post-Conciliar era. "In my lifetime, especially since Vatican II, I have seen more change in the Catholic Church than occurred during the preceding 450 years since the Reformation when we were a kind of 'fortress' Church," he said. "We are concerned about modern problems in a way we never were before and our approach to solving those problems is more open. The Church is more compassionate. It is praying better. It is more concerned about human problems. The Church is more honest about itself—that is, it views itself more as a 'pilgrim' Church, a divine institution without all the answers. In addition, Catholics have deeper interior motivation. They are doing their work in the Church out of dedication, concern, and conviction; not out of rote, routine, and habit. I am personally very happy about the state of the Church today. It is a great time to be a priest."

Of the contemporary problems confronting the Catholic Church today, such as birth control, marriage and divorce, priestly celibacy, abortion, and ecumenism, Hesburgh's thoughtful answers reflect a compassionate concern for the complex moral and social problems the Catholic Church must confront in a post-modern era. Hesburgh believes that most Catholics today are approaching the question of birth control from the perspective of responsible parenthood, and are trying to achieve this as efficaciously as possible with the means available. "I myself have been working very hard in forums where I have leverage such as the Rockefeller Foundation. I have encouraged the foundation to spend its money on research regarding ways and means of effectively controlling population rather than on handing out gadgets. We are now at a point where research in reproductive biology and the biochemistry of reproduction will give us a whole panoply of means to control population. These new methods will first of all be efficacious and reasonable in their cost, but even more importantly their diverse range would offer a variety of means acceptable to every culture and religion." Hesburgh believes that the Church will change its intractable stance on birth control. "There's going to be a great deal of future discussion on this and I wouldn't be at all surprised to see some modification in the Church's position."

Hesburgh believes there will also be a modification with respect to the Catholic Church's position on divorce. "There is no question in my mind that the sanctity and indissolubility of marriage contain the great Christian ideal, the very fruition of Christ's teachings. The dissolution of a marriage is a terribly tragic and unfortunate event for everyone involved. This tragic occurrence must be treated with enormous compassion and the Church must find a way to deal with it realistically. The Church must have a more benign approach, especially toward young people who have made an honest mistake and have their whole life before them. Official sanction of remarriage should be seriously considered by the Church because what the dissolution of marriage demands is a profound compassion. It may sound paradoxical to some but I firmly believe this can be done without weakening the Christian ideal that the measure of love in marriage is love without measure, that is, a man and woman take each other for better or worse, for richer or poorer, in sickness and in health, in order to bring each other to their eternal destiny."

With regard to priestly celibacy, Hesburgh sees no theological problem in permitting priests to marry. "I don't have any problem personally in seeing a priest married. Since all of the apostles were married with the exception of St. John, I don't believe there is a theological prohibition.'' According to Hesburgh, there may be situations where a priest would be better off if he were married. ''I've seen priests in the upper Amazon living in such desolate areas that they deteriorate mentally and physically because there is no one they can talk to. In this kind of primitive situation it would be better for a priest's very own salvation for him to be married. But even in less extreme conditions such as those found in country parishes where the quality of life in the rectory can become terribly impoverished and other problems arise as a result, marriage might be a solution to the isolation priests must endure.''

However, Hesburgh believes that celibacy is the ideal for priests. ''I am very much in favor of priestly celibacy, and if I were starting over again today I would still want to be a celibate priest. Celibacy is a sign that you have given yourself to God without reservation in order to serve men with an unreserved commitment. I have seen this in my own life where people with whom I have worked—many of them not Catholics—both in and out of government or public service—have been more struck by the fact that I was celibate than the fact that I said my breviary every day.''

Hesburgh's approach to abortion considers the problem in its full complexity. He believes that any resolution of this profound moral and social dilemma, so deeply felt on both sides of the issue, must be rooted in American pluralism. ''I think abortion is a very, very bad business. The Supreme Court is completely premature and overboard in its decision on abortion and it will eventually be forced to change it. The decision was, in fact, almost stupid—badly argued and badly written. I hate to think we'll have to wait as long as we did for the Court to reverse *Plessy v. Ferguson*, which in 1896 affirmed the separate but equal doctrine and was not overturned for nearly six decades until *Brown v. Board of Education* in 1954. I don't think we can wait that long, because abortion will meanwhile be running rampant, corroding the lives of many people, and driving our civilization deeper into materialism. I've seen this happen in Japan where the Americans introduced abortion widely after World War II as a birth control measure.''

''I am not sure what is the best way to resolve it,'' Hesburgh says. ''I don't get terribly excited or enthused about any of the presently proposed constitutional amendments. Of course it may be that an amendment is the best way to get at it. But I think the problem then will be to phrase the amendment in such a way that it is viable for not just Catholics and others who take a dim view of abortion. The amendment must be written so that it will be agreeable to the plurality of American points of view on abortion because there are many people of good will who are very much for abortion. The moral sensitivities of those who oppose abortion and those who support it must be fully considered.''

Hesburgh then went on to explain how a solution to the problem of abortion could be found in the context of the American constitutional experience with regard to the concept of religious freedom. ''It is analogous in a way to the situation the country was in when it began and there was a real problem concerning freedom of religion. How do you organize a society to guarantee that freedom? From the time of Constantine all religions were established by the state, receiving special status and benefits by virtue of that establishment. The Catholic religion, for example, was established throughout the entirety of Western Europe by emperors such as Constantine and Charlemagne. After the Reformation the Anglican religion was established by the English king, Henry VIII. In the Old Testament as well Judaism was a state religion. In America during the settlement of colonies, dissenters from the established religions came here for religious freedom, among them Quakers in Philadelphia, Catholics in Maryland, Puritans in Massachusetts. But they weren't here very long when ten of the 13 colonies made their particular dissident religion the established form of worship. The question then arose as to what should be done with those who disagreed with the established sect or who didn't want any religion at all.

"Well, the First Amendment with its first article on the disestablishment of religion provided one of the happiest constitutional solutions ever devised because it guaranteed a certain freedom of action with regard to religious worship and brought peace and unity out of an ancient and confusing historical problem fraught with great disunity, persecution, and prejudice. In a sense disestablishment was good for religion because by having no religion established by the state, all religions prospered since both the practice and the support of a particular creed are voluntary. The result is that you can't say the American government is anti-religious. All that can be said is that it doesn't support religion financially and doesn't support this religion against that one."

A similar solution with respect to abortion must be found, Hesburgh believes, because in his opinion the Supreme Court has "unwisely" placed the nation in a morally untenable position from which it must extricate itself. "Somehow I think we've got to find that kind of ingenious solution to abortion. Proponents of abortion are pushing it to the limit saying that abortions must be available on demand even at the moral expense of those who don't believe in it, a demand which I think is a grave offense against conscience. We've got to gather our good will to resolve this problem. I'm sure of one thing—the answer is not going to be the prohibition of abortion under any circumstances—even the Church doesn't say that. The other is that there isn't going to be free abortion on demand for just any frivolous reason, because I believe there is a fundamental right to life for the unborn which must be protected."

Hesburgh takes note of the prevailing uneasiness in the nation over the 1,500,000 abortions on demand every year. For example, a 1983 Gallup Poll indicated that 74 percent of Americans thought there should be restrictions on abortions, that is legal or illegal only under certain circumstances.

He knows that there is not a consensus in the nation for a total ban on abortion. Rather than have all or nothing, Hesburgh will support initiatives to prohibit abortion in the majority of cases, leaving exceptions in cases of rape, incest, or where the life of the mother is threatened.

Nevertheless, Hesburgh's opposition to abortion is unequivocal. "The fetus from the first moment of life is on the way, irrevocably, barring abortion, to full human life and human personhood." He contends that an answer to the philosophical issue of when personhood begins is not necessary in considering abortion as an abrogation of the moral order.

"What really persuades me of the basic immorality of induced abortion is a sign I once saw in Chinese above a cemetery in Hong Kong. It said: 'What you are I once was; what I am you soon will be.' A fetus could well say to us, 'What I am you once were; what you are I soon will be, if you let me,'" Hesburgh explains.[1]

While abortion was a prevailing campaign issue in the 1984 election campaign, a more fundamental debate emerged concerning the moral imperatives of the Catholic public servant in a pluralistic society.

The debate was intensified by two singular Catholic politicians in New York during the campaign: Geraldine Ferraro, Democratic vice presidential candidate, and Mario Cuomo, Governor of New York. Both held similar views on abortion: although personally opposed to abortion, they declared they would never impose their personal moral values on their constituents.

In a now-famous speech given at Notre Dame on September 13, 1984, Governor Cuomo addressed the tension between God and Caesar, i.e., religious belief and public morality. In regard to abortion, Cuomo strictly separated private morality from public morality. For Cuomo the failure of abortion was a private affair. "The failure here is not Caesar's. The failure is our failure, the failure of the people of God."

Yet Cuomo acknowledged that public morality was not created in a vacuum. "Our public morality . . .depends on a consensus view of right and wrong," he said.

Hesburgh challenged Cuomo's stand in an essay "Reflections on Cuomo: The Secret Consensus" published in the inaugural issue of *Notre Dame Journal of Law, Ethics & Public Policy* (1984).

Noting that with the First Amendment "religion became a matter of personal conviction in America," Hesburgh asserts that religious and political morality both influence each other. He contends it is "inconceivable that (politicians') religiously founded moral convictions will not affect their political lives."

For Hesburgh every fundamental political issue has a moral dimension whether it is the nuclear threat, human rights, poverty, housing, education, the Third World, drugs, environment, or abortion. This was evident in the 58-year-old debate over *Plessy v. Ferguson*, the 1896 Supreme Court decision which sanctioned the separate but equal doctrine for blacks.

Although *Plessy* was the law of the land, that did not prevent many from working against the law from within the law, according to Hesburgh. When *Brown v. Board of Education* overturned *Plessy* in 1954, a new American consensus was achieved. "Neither the consensus nor the change just happened; both were made to happen," Hesburgh writes.

Hesburgh contends that there is and has been a moral consensus for a more restrictive abortion law which was ignored by the Supreme Court in *Roe v. Wade*. In response to Cuomo's questions, Hesburgh declares: "If Catholics would help articulate this consensus favoring a more restrictive abortion law short of an absolute ban, Catholic politicians would no longer be able (or feel compelled) to say, 'I'm against abortion, but . . .'".

Hesburgh has also been concerned with the Vatican's recent proposal to assert its authority over doctrine in relation to Catholic universities worldwide. The proposal has taken the form of a schema ("Proposed Schema for a Pontifical Document on Catholic Universities") in which only those institutions who have a juridical relationship with the Vatican can be called "Catholic."

The juridical relationship would require that "doctrinal integrity and uprightness of life" be considered in the appointment and promotion of all professors. Further, teachers of theology must have "a mandate from the competent ecclesiastical authority" (e.g. a local bishop).

Hesburgh has opposed the extension of Vatican juridical control over American Catholic universities which are chartered by the state and governed by predominately lay boards of trustees. He reasons that a university is Catholic not because "of some pronouncement from afar or some intervention in its academic life during a supposed crisis but rather much more important realities that are internal to the life of the university not external to it."[2]

According to Hesburgh, those internal realities include the university's declared commitment to be Catholic as well as the faculty's and students' intellectual commitment to Catholicism. Moreover, Hesburgh says it is critical that theology remain autonomous within the Catholic university. If not, it will not be accepted as a university discipline in free dialogue with all other university disciplines.

Hesburgh affirms that Notre Dame has renewed its commitment to its Catholic character by continued emphasis on the importance of Catholic theology in the undergraduate curriculum, a public policy of preferential hiring for Catholic faculty, and concerted focus on research programs to reflect a Catholic value system and ethos.

In a critique of the schema sent to the Vatican's Congregation for Catholic Education, Hesburgh found diametric interests involved: "Under the legitimate rationale of trying to provide a model for Catholic institutions of higher education, (the proposed statement) adopts a univocal pattern irreconcilable with the form Catholic universities have taken in the United States." Hesburgh also noted that the schema would threaten Catholic institutions with the total loss of financial support from federal and state governments as well as private foundations. (Recent U.S. Supreme Court decisions determined that eligibility of Catholic institutions for federal aid must meet a two-part test: theology courses must be taught as academic disciplines not indoctrination exercises, and the curriculum must not be designed to inculcate religious beliefs.)[3]

Even beyond the potential financial loss is the loss of autonomy the university would suffer. "If church or state or any power outside the university can dictate who can teach and who can learn, the university is not free, and in fact, is not true university where the truth is sought and taught," says Hesburgh.[4]

On the occasion of Notre Dame's 125th anniversary in 1967, Hesburgh distinguished between the Catholic University and the Catholic Church: "The Catholic University might be said to be of the church as it serves both the church and the people of God, but it is certainly not the magisterium. It is not the church teaching, but a place—the only place—in which Catholics and others, on the highest level of intellectual inquiry, seek out the relevance of the Christian message to all the problems and opportunities that face modern man and his complex world."[5]

Ecumenism or the progress of the Christian religions toward unity is a movement which is of great concern to Hesburgh. He found great hope for this growing unity in the ecumenical advances made during and after the Second Vatican Council. However, he now believes the ecumenical movement must advance beyond its incipient stage to serious discussion and scholarship. Tentative tolerance is no longer enough. "Although great progress has been made," Hesburgh says, "we must get beyond handholding and merely being nice to one another. It is not enough to abstain from persecuting each other. Great tolerance is not sufficient. We must pray together more. The ancient emnities and misunderstandings must be put behind us once and for all. Christian unity is going to require a great deal of ecumenical conversation between scholars and the laborious working out of positions."

Hesburgh envisions a diverse Christian unity in which pluralism enriches the deposit of faith. "I look forward to a great single Christian church with a variety of practices within it in the way we have a plurality of practices within the Catholic Church," he says. "For example, today the Church has 16 different language rites even though it is called the Roman Catholic Church. There are many in the Roman Catholic Church who pray in Arabic, Greek, or some other language. The key is going to be *e pluribus unum*, many different points of view coming together in one, broad Christian Church.''

Pope Paul had such confidence in Hesburgh's ecumenical vision that in 1964 he asked him to take charge of establishing an ecumenical institute for advanced theological studies in Jerusalem. In doing so, Hesburgh built one of the most beautiful buildings constructed in Jerusalem since World War II according to Teddy Kolleck, mayor of Jerusalem. The institute, where Catholic, Orthodox, Anglican, and Protestant theologians convene for dialogue and scholarship, is located on the top of Tantur, an ancient hill covered with pine and olive trees lying between Jerusalem and Bethlehem.

Eventually Hesburgh envisions a similar ecumenical institute— perhaps at Notre Dame—for the great world religions where Jews, Muslims, Hindus, Buddhists, and others will meet and learn from each other in mutual respect and harmony. He has already encouraged this at the ecumenical institute in Jerusalem where seminars composed of Jewish, Arabic, Muslim, and Christian participants have been held.

As an example of his concern for ecumenism, Hesburgh initiated a dialogue between Christians and Jews at Notre Dame where he invited the well-known Jewish author and now Nobel Peace Prize winner Elie Wiesel to deliver a series of lectures on four Hassidic masters, charismatic representatives of the great Eastern European Jewish tradition of Hassidism founded in Poland in the middle of the 18th century. In June of 1978 ABC TV broadcast as part of its *Directions* series, a 30-minute conversation between Hesburgh and Wiesel with ABC News correspondent Frank Reynolds as moderator. The conversation focused on the piety and anguish of the Hassidic masters, the need to efface once and for all the ancient animus between Christians and Jews, and the urgent moral imperative summoning the modern world to confront the Holocaust in the very horror of its blasphemy against God and man.

Wiesel conceded to Reynolds that he was not a little surprised to find himself lecturing at a Catholic university. "In the middle of a Catholic campus. . .the response here was to me a surprise," he said. "I didn't expect to see myself here. At one point in my lecture I stopped and said, 'What am I doing here?'" Wiesel's own experience had taught him that he was an alien—even an enemy—among Christians and he recalled that as a child he had been beaten up by Christian friends at Christmas and Easter.

"In my little town I didn't even know that the Jews and Christians believed in the same God," he continued. "I thought that Christians only believed in Jesus. I didn't know that they were believing in my God. Why? Because we were so totally different. We lived in the same town, but yet I never saw a church, if I saw a priest, I'd run away, for good reasons. You know, we have had our experiences."

Hesburgh said that as a young boy growing up in Syracuse and attending parochial school he knew mostly Catholics and thought of Jews as "being somewhat different. . .which of course they are and should be. But you don't always think of someone different in those days as being a good thing. It was generally thought of being a bad thing. They're not like us, if you will. . .Why can't everybody be like us?"

In the program Hesburgh referred to an Hassidic Midrash which suggests that if one bases his own identity on the difference between himself and others, then that person will never be himself: "If I am what I am because you are what you are, then you are not you, and I am not I." It is this paradox, according to Hesburgh, which is at the center of ecumenism, and indeed, the reconciliation of Christians and Jews.

The quest for unity among men and religions finds its end in what Hesburgh calls "the vital center which embraces contraries." He elucidated upon this during the program in entreating a return to the "transcendental center which is the holy name of God." "If we could get back to that center," he declared, "we would be amazed how close Jews and Muslims and Christians would be because we are all sons of Abraham, we all worship the God of Abraham, Isaac, and Jacob. We are all religions of the book—the Word of God impinging on human history. That is the vital center which draws us together, the common center which calls us into unity."

CHAPTER 12
MELCHIZEDEK'S MASTERFUL
MEDIATOR: A PRIEST FOREVER

Former Yale President Kingman Brewster recalls that in the summer of 1975 at the quinquennial meeting of the International Association of Universities in Moscow it was Father Hesburgh's warm diplomatic presence which enabled Stanford University President Richard Lyman and himself to make contact with key Soviet officials. "Who should put President Lyman and myself in touch with the Minister of Higher Education, the director of *Tass*, and the former head of the Russian atomic energy program? None other than Father Ted. It struck me as very amusing that these secular progressive university presidents from Yale and Stanford should have to find that their best ambassador in the precincts of the Kremlin was this Catholic priest who was the president of Notre Dame. This came about of course because Father Ted was deputized as the Pope's representative at the International Atomic Energy Agency in Vienna and therefore came to know all these characters."

"And like the rest of us," Brewster continued, "they developed a great deal of confidence in him in spite of their completely opposite ideological positions. Ted has always been amused by his role in that regard. I think this is typical of his role in the society in general. That is, he has been a strong fighter for causes he believes in yet at the same time a bridge builder also. He is the kind of person who is trusted by people who don't usually trust each other."

"It was also fun to watch him as a master of small talk in order to get everyone relaxed so we could discuss serious issues. This incident is typical of the ecumenical role he plays in society, a diplomatic and mediating role which extends throughout the world."

Jim Hesburgh recalls another such diplomatic mediation his brother performed at a meeting of the International Atomic Energy Agency in which a reconciliation was achieved between representatives of the East and West by virtue of Hesburgh's conciliatory maneuvering among the delegates, a reconciliation culminating in a Mass celebrated by Franz Cardinal Koenig in Stephansdom, Vienna's Cathedral, and attended by the mutually hostile representatives.

"When Ted was representing the Vatican at the International Atomic Energy Agency in Vienna along with Frank Folsom of RCA, he took more than casual notice that all of the delegates would divide up into little camps, so to speak, of East and West, Communist and non-Communist. Since his basic philosophy is that you cannot understand people or get them to understand you unless you can communicate with them, he went out of his way to meet with the Soviet delegation. This caused much consternation and people started saying, 'What is this priest doing representing the Vatican and getting buddy-buddy with the Russians?'

"Well, to break the ice Ted started giving them all nick-names, calling one of the Russians 'Boston Blackie.' As a result, he became good friends with them, including the head of the Soviet delegation, Vassily Emelyanov. At cocktail parties he would come to them in their isolated corner and discuss their philosophy with them. Eventually, in addition to the cocktail parties the Russians started attending the Mass he always celebrated with the Vienna Boy's Choir."

"One year he invited delegates from the other Communist nations as well, and because of it started receiving criticism from Western delegations, especially the British who asked how he could do such a thing. He was strongly advised not to continue but he went ahead and did it anyway. Not only that, he translated the Mass and sermon into Russian. On the night before, the delegates from Eastern and Western blocs had split right down the middle over a certain issue. Inviting the delegates to his hotel room, Ted acted as an intermediary and was able to get the key representatives from both sides to discuss and resolve the impasse. On Sunday morning, leaders of both sides walked down the center aisle of the Cathedral together."

To many observers it appears that Hesburgh may be one of those gifted individuals in the Church best prepared to assuage the separation between the sacred and profane. In the words of Dr. Franklin Murphy: "When the Church was in deep trouble in the Middle Ages someone came along and his name was Thomas Aquinas. He built a bridge between the Aristotelian scientific world and theology at a very critical point in the life of the Church. It permitted the Church to maintain a high degree of religious commitment and philosophy and yet relate to the real world as it was emerging."

Hesburgh's talent for diplomacy is exemplified in his concern for the Nuclear Age.

In 1982, Jonathan Schell published a book called *The Fate of the Earth* in which he assessed the destructive cataclysm which would be wrought by a nuclear war. In the book he writes that "nuclear weapons are unique in that they attack the support systems of life at every level."[1] The fatal consequence is that the earth—the largest of life's support systems—would be irrevocably impaired by nuclear war.[2]

Schell also states that the biblical mandate "Be fruitful and multiply" is not only biological: "The nuclear peril makes all of us, whether we have children of our own or not, the parents of all future generations."[3] Schell concludes that as parental love is unconditional so should be our concern for the fate of the earth.

Hesburgh read the book and was deeply moved and influenced by it. Beginning in the early 1980's, Hesburgh had already begun curtailing his activities outside the university in order to address the nuclear peril and find practical ways to eliminate it.

As he told Robert Schmuhl in *The University of Notre Dame: A Contemporary Portrait:*[4] "It suddenly struck me—I knew it all the time but there is a difference between knowing something and being struck by it—that everything else that I've been working on all my life would be literally wiped out by a nuclear attack."

"It would be the end of everything. It would be the end of all the great institutions, such as the universities, governments, libraries, and families. Everything would be gone. Our future would be gone and with it everybody else's future—the future's future."

Much of Hesburgh's effort has been to bring together world religious leaders and distinguished scientists from the five major nuclear powers including the United States and the Soviet Union. In order to foster this interchange, Hesburgh has created at Notre Dame an Institute for International Peace Studies. The Institute was established in December 1985 with a $6 million gift from Joan Kroc, widow of Ray Kroc, the founder of the McDonald's Restaurant chain.

The Institute creates peace fellowships for young scholars of several nations including the Soviet Union and the People's Republic of China. It will consolidate existing academic courses into a comprehensive program of peace studies for Notre Dame undergraduate students. In addition, a multidisciplinary research program will explore specific aspects of the relationship between human rights, justice and peace.

Director of the Institute is John J. Gilligan, former governor of Ohio. Hesburgh chairs the international advisory board, which includes Carols Chagas, president of the Vatican's Pontifical Academy of Sciences; Gu Yi Jian, secretary general of the Chinese Academy of Sciences; Franz Cardinal Koenig, former archbishop of Vienna; Joseph Cardinal Bernardin, archbishop of Chicago.

Other board members include Robert S. McNamara, former U.S. Secretary of Defense; Cyrus Vance, former U.S. Secretary of State; Gerard C. Smith, chief negotiator of the SALT I Treaty; John C. Steinbruner, director of the Brookings Institution's foreign study program; Yevgeny Velikhov, vice president of the Soviet Academy of Sciences; Roald Z. Sagdeev, director of the Institute for Space Research for the Soviet Academy of Sciences; James E. Muller, cofounder of the Physicians for Social Responsibility; and Wolfgang K. H. Panofsky, director emeritus of the Stanford Linear Accelerator Center.

A fair criticism of the advisory board's makeup is that it represents almost exclusively liberal viewpoints on arms control and nuclear weapons. To be truly effective and achieve the needed consensus for pragmatic approaches to arms control, discerning conservative viewpoints should have been included. For example, a Henry Kissinger or James Schlesinger could provide a perspective on how a well-balanced military deterrence policy can induce arms control and enhance stability between the United States and the Soviet Union.

"I have always said that here is another one of those moments in history where tradition comes right up against a rush of change. Now what is needed are mediators which Aquinas was. He was a philosophical mediator. Now here is Ted, who will tell you and everyone else—'I am a priest first and foremost.' So there should be no question about his commitment to his faith. But with all of that here is a man who has one foot planted right in the middle of the 21st century, who has the respect, affection, and admiration of non-Catholics, Jews, Protestants, Muslims, Hindus. He should be used or have the opportunity to be encouraged to play this Aquinas-type role, to build that bridge. Why they haven't recognized this, I'll never know—they're blind."

Andrew Greeley concurs, saying "he is probably the most qualified individual in the Church to play this Aquinas-type role." However, it is as a priest that Hesburgh finds the fruition of his gifts.

It means being a mediator," says Hesburgh. "You have to stand between God and man and all that it involves, between sin and goodness, between ignorance and knowledge, between being uncared for and caring, standing in a thousand human situations between God and men, trying to bring the message of God to man and man's petitions to God. It means you have to offer sacrifice as a priest for the salvation of the whole world every day. You have to be committed to the salvation of the world and all that it entails—very variegated things. It means many temporal things such as civil rights, human justice, human and world development, things I've spent my life doing, things that I don't think are unrelated to my being a priest. I think education is a very priestly activity. I think anything bringing us from ignorance to knowledge would hopefully be seen as a priestly activity. Being a priest, I guess, means being totally committed to God and totally committed to man and standing between them both, trying to be reasonably close to God, which we never do as well as we should, and being reasonably close to man, which is much easier." "You are a priest forever, according to the order of Melchizedek," is one of the majestic declaratives of the Old Testament, and truly, Theodore Martin Hesburgh is one of Melchizedek's masterful mediators.

Footnotes

Chapter 3

1. Thomas Schlereth, *The University of Notre Dame: A Portrait of Its History and Campus.* New York/London: University of Notre Dame Press, 1975. p. 30
2. Ibid., p. 10.
3. Ibid., p. 32.
4. Ibid., p. 32.
5. Ibid., p. 32.
6. Ibid., p. 32.
7. Ibid., p. 57.
8. Ibid., pp. 122-123.
9. Ibid., p. 146.
10. Ibid., p. 145.
11. Ibid., p. 170.
12. Ibid., pp. 178-181.
13. Ibid., p. 181.
14. Ibid., p. 198.
15. Ibid., p. 196.
16. Ibid., p. 196.
17. Ibid., p. 123.
18. Ibid., p. 122.
19. Ibid., p. 19.
20. Ibid., p. 19.
21. Ibid., p. 123.
22. Ibid., p. 124.
23. Ibid., p. 124

Chapter 4

1. Thomas R. Horton, Ed., *What Works For Me,* New York: Random House, 1986, p. 156.
2. Ibid., p. 157.
3. Ibid., p. 157.
4. Ibid., p. 162.
5. Ibid., p. 165.
6. Ibid., p. 158.
7. Ibid., p. 158.
8. Hesburgh, "The University President," *The Hesburgh Papers: Higher Values in Higher Education,* pp. 8-9.
9. Hesburgh, "Science and Technology in Modern Perspective," *The Hesburgh Papers,* Sheed, Andrews, McMeel, Kansas City, 1979, pp. 97-98.
10. Ibid.

11. Thomas J. Schlereth, "The University of Notre Dame: A Portrait of Its History and Campus," Notre Dame/London: University of Notre Dame Press: 1975, p. 205.
12. Ibid., p. 208.
13. Ibid., pp. 208-209.
14. Ibid., p. 209.
15. Ibid., p. 213.
16. Ibid., p. 214.

Chapter 5

1. Civil disobedience—no matter how cogent the cause—carries with it the attendant risk of a discord so pervasive that society itself may become uncivil. Alexander Bickel, the great scholar of constitutional law at Yale, reflected upon the student demonstrations of the 60's shortly before his death in 1974. In his book *The Morality of Consent,* Bickel censured those in charge of the nation's universities for not coming to terms with the hazardous proliferation of disrupting demonstrations on the campuses. "[Civil] disobedience, even if legitimate in every other way, must not be allowed to become epidemic," he advised. "Individuals are under a duty to ration themselves, to assess occasions in terms of their relative as well as absolute importance . . . For disobedience is attended by the overhanging threat of anarchy. We did not ration ourselves in disobedience, and those in authority in the universities in the late sixties imposed no rationing. Coming as the third wave of massive disobedience movements in fifteen years, the demonstrations of the late sixties, including the most peaceable and legitimate ones of all, carried the clear and present danger of anarchy." Bickel, *The Morality of Consent,* Yale University Press, 1975, p. 119.
2. Connelly, Joel R. and Dooley, Howard J., *Hesburgh's Notre Dame: Triumph in Transition,* Hawthorn Books, Inc., New York, 1972; p. 296.

Chapter 6

1. Foster Rhea Dulles. *The Civil Rights Commission: 1957-1965,* Michigan State University Press, 1968, pp. 1-2.
2. Dulles quoting Sherman Adams *Firsthand Report; The Story of the Eisenhower Administration.* Greenwood, 1975, p. 17.
3. Ibid., p. 18.
4. Ibid., p. 32.
5. Ibid., p. 34.
6. Ibid., p. 35.
7. Ibid., p. 39.

Chapter 7

1. Jonathan Schell, *The Time of Illusion,* NY, Vantage Books, 1976.

Chapter 9

1. Houck, John W. and Williams, Oliver F. eds., *Co-Creation and Capitalism: John Paul II's Laborem Exercens*, Washington, D.C.: University of America Press, 1983, p. 13.
2. Ibid., p. 171.
3. Theodore M. Hesburgh C.S.C., *The Humane Imperative: A Challenge for the Year 2000*. New Haven & London: Yale University Press, 1974. p. 13.
4. Ibid., p. 50.
5. Ibid., p. 52.
6. Ibid., p. 52-55.
7. Jose Napoleon Duarte, *Duarte, My Story*, G.P. Putman's Sons, 1986. NY, pp. 9-10.
8. Ibid., pp. 15-16.

Chapter 10

1. Hesburgh, "Letter of Transmittal" Select Commission on Immigration and Refugee Policy, Second Semi-Annual Report to Congress, October 1980, v.
2. Ibid., v.
3. Ibid., v.
4. Ibid., vi.
5. Lawrence H. Fuchs, "Immigration Reform in 1911 and 1981: The Role of the Select Commissions," *Journal of American Ethnic History*, Fall 1983, Vol. 3, No. 1, p. 58, 65.
6. Ibid., p. 62-63.
7. Ibid., p. 66.
8. Hesburgh, U.S. Immigration Policy and the National Interest, the Final Report and Recommendations of the Select Commission on Immigration and Refugee Policy, March 1, 1981, xvii, 3.
9. Fuchs, op. cit. pp. 66-69.
10. Ibid., pp. 69-72.
11. Hesburgh, U.S. Immigration Policy and the National Interest, pp. 4-5.
12. Fuchs, op. cit. pp. 72-73.
13. Hesburgh, U.S. Immigration Policy and the National Interest, p. 15.
14. Ibid., p. 16.
15. Fuchs, op. cit. pp. 76-78.
16. Hesburgh, U.S. Immigration Policy and the National Interest, pp. xxi, 2.

Chapter 11

1. Hesburgh. *The Sunday Visitor.* "Pro Life from the Social Justice Perspective." January 18, 1981. pp. 6-7.
2. Hesburgh. *America.* "The Vatican and American Catholic Higher Education." November 1, 1986. p.61.
3. *Notre Dame Magazine*, Summer 1986, p. 8.

4. "The Vatican and American Catholic Higher Education" *America*, November 1, 1986. p. 62.
5. "The Vision of the Catholic University in the World Today." *The Hesburgh Papers: Higher Values in Higher Education.* Kansas City: Andrews and McMeel, Inc., 1979, p. 41.

Chapter 12

1. Jonathan Schell, *The Fate of the Earth*, New York: Alfred Knopf, 1982, p. 23.
2. Ibid., p. 23.
3. Ibid., p. 175.
4. Robert Schmuhl, *The University of Notre Dame: A Contemporary Portrait*, Notre Dame: University of Notre Dame Press, 1986, p. 175.